An Angel Called Mervín

JENNIFER REES LARCOMBE

An Angel
Called Mervin

The Christian Story through Celestial Eyes

GRAND RAPIDS, MICHIGAN 49530 USA

WWW.ZONDERVAN.COM

Marshall Pickering is an Imprint of
HarperCollins*Religious*
Part of HarperCollins*Publishers*
77–85 Fulham Palace Road, London W6 8JB

First published in Great Britain in 1999
by Marshall Pickering

1 3 5 7 9 10 8 6 4 2

Jennifer Rees Larcombe asserts the moral right to be
identified as the author of this work

A catalogue record for this book
is available from the British Library

ISBN 0 551 03212 X

Printed and bound in Great Britain by
Caledonian International Book Manufacturing Ltd, Glasgow

Contents

To Violet and Diana

Preface

During the last four years, whenever I've mentioned that I was writing a book about angels, people have often said, 'Really? Well, I'm quite sure I saw one once.' There have indeed been many well-documented 'sightings' in recent years, on which some very absorbing books have been based. Although I am deeply interested in angels, I did not want to write that kind of book. Instead I wanted to share my fascination with what the Bible tells us about these 'celestial beings' and how they interact with human beings. I've used an imaginary character called Mervin who is 'the Principal of the Celestial Training School For Newly Created Angels'.

It might seem as if I have trodden into the realms of fantasy and produced a work of fiction, but all the incidents and concepts in the story are based on the Bible, and I have given references so that readers can check for themselves!

Followers of Jesus must believe in the existence and constant intervention of angels in our lives, because Jesus Himself did. He spoke of them and encountered them often. Angels and their activities are mentioned directly nearly 300 times throughout the Bible from Genesis to Revelation, and indirectly they are referred to at least 600 times.

I also wanted to write about spiritual warfare, because I think we often have the impression that it's about humans fighting the powers of darkness. I believe spiritual warfare is all about holy angels fighting fallen angels, but it is human faith which always decides which side wins in each skirmish.

But this book is not just about angels. I've tried to tell the whole story of the Bible and God's dealings with people through angelic eyes, as if they were looking down from Heaven and watching everything that happened on earth, adding their own comments and discussing the events as they unfolded.

On a personal note, I have to say that I have enjoyed writing this book more than any other I've ever written. I think it's my twenty-third! It's taken me longer than any other because the last three years of my life have definitely been the hardest and most stressful. Writing and researching for *An Angel Called Mervin* has encouraged my faith in God like nothing else, and it's helped me to see all the nasty events of my life in proportion and from the viewpoint of Heaven and eternity. So, if I am the only person whom it blesses, it will still have been worth all the hard work! But I long that it will also bless others, particularly those who are going through difficult times.

Jennifer Rees Larcombe

Prologue

This is the transcript of the inauguration lecture delivered on the first day of term by an angel called Mervin, the Principal of the Celestial Training School For Newly Created Angels.

Right! Thanks for that applause, but settle down now, fold your wings and put your harps under your chairs. Music lessons come later in the course, and I can't stand tinkering and plucking while I talk.

At the moment you may well be sitting there wondering why you've been created, when you know that the universe is already teeming with billions of us angels. There's no heavenly reason, but there is an earthly one – the population explosion! Down there on earth they're breeding like rabbits these days, and in order to provide each newly born Earth Child with a Guardian Angel, the Mighty One has to create a new batch every now and again to keep pace with the human birthrate. It's as simple as that![1]

You're probably also wondering who I am, so I'll introduce myself.

Well, I'm not a high-ranking celestial being, like the cherubim, the seraphim or the Archangel – I'm just a plain, ordinary, working-class angel. Billions of light years ago I was given a little star to look after somewhere on the far side of the Milky Way. It was a lovely little place, until it decided to explode and become a shooting star – that was my job blown to smithereens! So I was redundant, after all those years of hard work! But now I've been relocated and given the task of turning you lot into useful beings ready to serve the Mighty One, in whatever way He chooses. Looking at you all, it's obvious that I've got a lot of hard work in front of me, and the sooner we make a start the better.

Next, you'll want to know what angels *do*. Believe me, we *don't* sit around on clouds playing harps all the time – whatever they may think down on Earth. We work hard and we're highly organized but, as I'm sure you've noticed, we laugh a lot.[2] In fact, Heaven's full of laughter, and you'll miss it badly when you get sent down to Earth. They don't seem to laugh much down there. I'll explain the reason for that later.

✽

There are countless departments in Heaven, and once I've finished with you, you could be drafted to any one of them – according to the way you shape up during training.

For instance, there are the Messenger Angels under the leadership of Gabriel.[3] The Mighty One uses them to run His errands and deliver His messages all over the universe.[4]

Gabriel gets all the plum jobs, of course, but the rest of them are kept very busy too. Those Messengers are always in a hurry, darting and dashing between Earth and Heaven. It's hard work, but they're never bored!

Sometimes they 'appear' to Earthlings and deliver their messages in an audible voice,[5] but those Earthlings can be so irritating! Instead of getting on and obeying orders instantly like any self-respecting angel, they often waste vital time by protesting that the angel was only a figment of their imagination, or the result of too much alcohol or cheese for supper! So, generally, the Messengers just 'thought-plant'[6] their despatches, and the Earthlings never realize they've been 'visited' at all.

The lowest-grade angels in the Messenger Division are simply posted all over the earth as Watchers,[7] reporting back up here when they see anything which needs special attention.

Then there are the Guardian Angels, whom I've already mentioned. They're sometimes called Ministering Spirits.[8] Promotion prospects are good in that department because a successful Guardian could be asked to oversee a church,[9] a town or even a nation,[10] but the vast majority of the lads in that division just have one Earthling to look after. As I've already told you, each Earthling baby is assigned their own personal Guardian the moment they're born.[11] That's probably the way you'll start your career, and it can be quite a nice little job really, so long as you're given a quiet, well-behaved child, but some of them can be horrors. I've seen many a promising young angel become totally stressed out by some of those Earth-kids (or they *would* be, if angels *could* be stressed out!). You wouldn't believe some of the things those children do down there. I doubt if the human race would have survived at all without us angels to haul them out of ponds, pull them back from the edge of cliffs and stand between them and sinister strangers. Of course, you won't always succeed in protecting them, or even manage to keep them alive long enough to mature into adults, because there's always one of the 'Other Sort of Angel' posted on each case as well. But I'll tell you all about them and their antics later. (By the way, don't go thinking that Earth is a lovely, peaceful place – it's a battle-ground down there. Believe me, it's *all-out war* between us and 'the Others').[12]

While I'm talking of the Guardians, I probably ought to warn you that some of them come back up here heartbroken (well, they *would* be if we angels had hearts to break).[13] You just wouldn't believe some of the things that adult Earthlings do to their children – the cruelty, the abuse, the exploitation! When you learn what the Mighty One's got in store for those abusing adults, you'll think it would be better for them to fall into one of Earth's oceans right now, with a lump of granite tied round their necks.[14] Some of them are going to get a big shock when they realize that all the terrible things they did in secret are known so publicly up here!

When Earthlings reach a certain age they can choose to reject the assistance of their Guardian and 'do their own thing' (as they say on Earth), or they can opt into our system, in which case they will have at least one of us in constant attendance for the rest of their lives.[15]

Now, I wouldn't want you to think that the Mighty One loses interest completely in the Earthlings who reject Him and dismiss their Guardians. No way! Every time another Earthling prays for them, the Mighty One despatches an angel from a small but highly trained squad known as the Evangels.[16] Their orders are to encourage the rebellious Earthlings to go where they will hear about the Mighty One and His continuing love and concern for them.[17] Very important function, those Evangels have. The Mighty One values them very highly.

Of course, all plain, working-class angels like me would love to be promoted to the rank of Warrior Angel.[18] You'll recognize them by their swords – and their size. Believe me, they're *big*. If you meet one, stand to attention, fold your wings neatly and keep your mouth shut. It's not worth messing with those Warriors – they're too big! The Archangel Michael himself is their Chief of Staff.[19] Of course, he's the Senior Angel up here in Heaven. The 'Big Guys' (that's what the rest of us call the Warriors) are only *one* of Michael's responsibilities.

You know, it sometimes makes us laugh when we hear Earthling mothers describe their fat, pink babies as 'little angels'. If they only knew the fierce, military appearance of a fully armed Warrior they certainly wouldn't confuse him with a bare-bottomed, thumb-sucking Earth Infant! Big Guys look so terrifying that they are hardly ever allowed to be seen by Earthlings – the Mighty One is too kind to frighten humans that much!

There are four very high-ranking Warriors who control the weather down there on Earth.[20] Another is in charge of the sea,[21] and another manages fire.[22] The rest of the Big Guys, 'the Host of Heaven', protect Earthlings who ask the Mighty One for help and fight His enemies.[23]

Even more terrifying are the Angels of Judgement (sometimes known as the Reapers).[24] There are seven of them,[25] and their leader is known as the Angel of Death.[26] I think you're a bit too newly created to know much about him just yet. Grim, he is – very grim indeed!

Now I think it's high time I told you about the highest form of heavenly being, the Cherubs.[27] And they are definitely *not* fat babies either! The Cherubim are so gigantic that if you even tried to peep at them, their light would dazzle you. The job of the Cherubim is to stay close to the Mighty One, supporting His throne on their great shoulders.[28]

The Seraphim are almost as beautiful, and we call them the 'Burning Ones' because of their gorgeous fiery colours. You'll always be able to spot them easily, because they have six wings.[29] To join that lot you have to be able to 'sing like an angel' (as they say on Earth), manage a harp well, and possibly a trumpet too. The Seraphim's responsibility is to circle the Mighty One Himself and to worship Him continuously.[30] They have a lovely job – every angel yearns for the honour of doing that.

There are many other departments in Heaven, but I think that's enough for your small heads at the moment. We angels aren't expected to know everything,[31] we were simply created to serve the Mighty One – whatever Earthlings may think.

✱

Actually, they have some very odd ideas about angels down there. For a start, they don't have a clue about what we look like. Of course, they *think* they know, and you'll have a good laugh when you're first sent to Earth and you see some of the pictures and statues that they've made of us. They either make us look like overweight babies (minus a nappy) or pious-looking, golden-haired females suffering from advanced anorexia. It's even more insulting when they give us huge, feathery wings and make us look like multicoloured super-birds flapping our way round the universe. Yes, of course we have wings, but they're not for flapping – we glide effortlessly through the cosmos and at such high speed that we can be anywhere almost instantly.[32] But we have arms and hands too – just having wings would be most irritating.[33] By the way, if a group of you are ever sent to appear on Earth together, do remember that the sound of our wings is almost deafening to their ears, like the roar of a stormy ocean or the sound of a vast army on the march.[34] Rainbow-coloured birds indeed!

There was once an Earthling called John who was allowed up here to have a look round Heaven. When he went back down again he said we looked as if we were wearing clouds like grand robes, we had rainbows round our heads, our faces shone like the sun and our legs looked like pillars of shooting flame.[35] Poor man – he did his best, but you can see what a pathetically limited description that is!

✱

It will probably be a long time before any of you get sent down to Earth, but just in case there's a sudden crisis and you're posted in an emergency, here are a few rules for 'Earth visits'. Take them down carefully and learn them by heart. We angels can make silly mistakes sometimes,[36] even though we can't sin deliberately[37] these days.

Rule 1: Try to stay invisible. Our job is to focus attention on the Mighty One and never on ourselves. Seeing one of us can distract humans and send them half mad with terror. So our Majestic Master will most likely send you to help, comfort, rescue or protect your Earthling invisibly. If you're sent with a message, plant it in their minds. If they won't take any notice, then speak audibly, but remember that our voices sound terrifyingly loud to them.

Rule 2: Be careful that they don't worship you.[38] Earthlings have a ridiculous tendency to worship anything and everything rather than the Mighty One Himself.[39] So often, when one of us has appeared to some ordinary Earthling with a simple little message, all the other Earthlings for miles around turn the spot into a shrine for ever afterwards, and even start praying to us! Dreadful idea!

Rule 3: Go in disguise. When you're specifically told to appear, rather than just doing your job invisibly, try to look as much like an Earthling as possible.[40] Angels were not created to flaunt themselves, so, unless it's strictly necessary, glittering light, blazing auras and swirling sunbeams are nothing but showing off. Most often we are allowed to appear to Earthlings when they're in trouble, and the last thing they'll want at a time like that is to be dazzled by our full ceremonial dress.

Rule 4: Scare off enemies. Quite often when we are protecting Earthlings we appear to their enemies but stay invisible to our charges. Would-be robbers, rapists or murderers have often been too scared to attack because they have seen our charges surrounded by 'tall men', even though they were, humanly speaking, quite alone![41] That kind of assignment is such fun!

Rule 5: Learn to merge. Don't forget that when you're appearing as a human in certain parts of the world, people expect angels to have golden hair, white skin and blue eyes. On the other hand, if you appeared like that in Africa, Asia or Latin America you would upset people horribly. And remember to use the right language and the local dialect. Here in Heaven, of course, we speak the universal language of angels,[42] but the gift of using and understanding that language is only given to very few on Earth. You will find that you can do your job far more effectively if the human feels comfortable with you.

Rule 6: *Emphasize important messages.* If it's vital that an Earthling takes notice of your message, the Mighty One will instruct you to impress him or her by appearing as the Earthling *thinks* angels *should* look – shimmering lights, dazzling robes, wings, halo – the lot. It's hard to make Earthlings take any notice of messages from Heaven; so a bit of a shock does grab their attention. If you *do* go in full regalia, remember that you'll always have to open the interview with the standard line, 'Fear not.'[43] They are always terrified of an angel in full plumage because we look gigantic to them.

Rule 7: *Don't let the Earthling try to make a relationship.* They will try to get sociable, so never tell them your name[44] – only Gabriel and Michael are allowed to do that. Do your job and then disappear. Don't hang around making friends. Angels weren't created to be friends – just to serve. Don't say fatuous things like, 'You can call me any time. I'm your own angel and I'll always be there for you.' Ridiculous! If you're their Guardian, of course you're always there for them, but they can't call you up at will, like a genie in a fairy story. You can only speak to them when the Mighty One gives you permission. You can't even intervene to help them unless they, or someone else, prays to Him first. It's only then that He activates us.[45]

Rule 8: *Watch out for Earthlings who get too fascinated by angels*[46] and who develop a consuming desire for an 'appearance'. This kind of obsession takes their attention off the Mighty One and puts them in grave danger too. Our enemies, the dark angels, love dressing up as angels of light and giving Earthlings phoney messages from the Mighty One.[47]

Rule 9: *Remember that children and animals are far more likely to see us than adult Earthlings are.*[48] Animals are usually afraid, but children never are. That is why the Mighty One so often uses us to comfort children. Generally you will be told to go to them looking like a child of about their own age, but really your appearance makes little difference to a child, because they're always pleased to see you. They tell adults they saw 'a pretty lady' or 'a kind man' or talk about 'my secret friend', and adults chuckle indulgently. Sad to say, as children grow up they, too, begin to think that the angels they saw were only 'make believe'. All the same, most Earth Children probably see us angels in one form or another before they grow too old to be susceptible to the supernatural.

Rule 10: Move with the times. We used to ride chariots and horses of fire,[49] but these days you'll be a lot less conspicuous driving a car, lorry or motorbike! You'll have to ride on trains and buses with your charges too, but the best fun of all is sitting astride a great aircraft when your Earthlings are on board. We angels love that – the wind blows our hair and billows our robes out behind us. We've even taken humans into orbit in space capsules and walked with them on the Moon.

There is one last vital thing that you must get firmly into your head, right from the start. Angels were not created to show initiative – we were created to serve our Mighty Master. He rules the universe; and angels, however powerful and glorious they may be, are simply the tools that He uses to carry out His plans.

But that's enough of all that. It's high time we moved on to something far more interesting.

✸

Your reason for existing at all is to please the Mighty One – to serve Him, to obey His every wish and, most important of all, to worship Him.[50] That's why you've all been issued with those wretched harps you keep fidgeting with. Leave them alone while I'm talking! I need to think clearly – this is the vital bit of my lecture.

First, I must warn you. Although it's unlikely that you'll get very close to the Mighty One for a while, you must know how to behave, should you be summoned to His presence. If He speaks to you, you *have* to cover your face with your wings and say, 'Holy, Holy, Holy.'[51] You must remember that the Mighty One is holy – so holy that we can't look into His face, because we're only angels.[52]

He's not only Holy, He's all powerful.[53] He holds the entire universe together. Just one word from Him, and everything would be instantly annihilated – including *you*.

He's also vast. When you see Him sitting on His throne, you're only seeing a tiny part of Him. He's able to be everywhere in the universe at once.[54] It's pointless trying to keep anything from Him, because He knows everything that's happening to every creature[55] or human on Earth – what they are doing and thinking[56] – and the same applies to all Good and Bad Angels as well. He's so awesome that not even Michael or Gabriel, the greatest angels of all, can understand Him.

And the part that we angels find most confusing of all is that not only is He holy, supremely powerful, all knowing, everywhere at once, the source of all life, the Creator of everything, but – and I find this very hard to say – He's also … *Love*. Now, you won't understand what that word means. No angel ever can, because we weren't created to love – just to serve.

We feel that being Love is the Mighty One's greatest problem. If only He wasn't Love, the Universe would be so much easier to manage – Bad Angels and people could be instantly destroyed so that the good ones could relax. But love makes everything so untidy. Well, that's what we angels think, anyway – not that we were created to think, just to serve.

The trouble is that Love seems to make the Mighty One so vulnerable.[57] He wants the ones He loves to be completely happy, and only ever wants the best for them, but that can be most awkward when what they want clashes with what He can see is best for them. Even more unfortunate, Love needs to be loved in return, and that's changed the entire dynamics of the world.[58]

Naturally, we angels didn't know that the Mighty One was Love – not at first. We watched Him creating planets, suns and stars – having endless fun juggling about with them and throwing them around in space.[59] He seemed quite happy for billions of years, forming them into intricate patterns, building constellations and galaxies galore – and all the while he was adding more wonders to Heaven itself. There isn't a single angel who's ever had time to explore all of Heaven's extremities. It's so big that its borders are limitless. It literally goes on for ever! He put an angel in charge of each of those stars. The higher their status, the bigger the star they were given.

Yes? You had your hand up? Quite right – that is why my star was so small!

Notes

1. This is only 'artistic licence' and not strictly true. All angels – both holy ones and fallen ones – were created by God at one time.
2. Heb. 12:22.

3. Dan. 4:13.
4. Dan. 8:15–16.
5. Acts 10:1–6.
6. 1 Kings 13:1.
7. Isa. 62:6.
8. Heb. 1:14.
9. Rev. 2:1.
10. Dan. 12:1.
11. Matt. 18:10.
12. Rev. 12:7–8.
13. Rev. 21:4.
14. Matt. 18:6.
15. Ps. 91:11–12.
16. Rev. 14:6.
17. Acts 8:26.
18. Joel 3:11.
19. Rev. 12:7.
20. Rev. 7:1.
21. Rev. 16:5.
22. Rev. 8:7.
23. 2 Kings 6:17.
24. Matt. 13:29; Rev. 14:15–19.
25. Rev. 8:6–7.
26. 2 Sam. 24:16–17.
27. Mentioned 91 times in the Bible and best described in Ezek. 1. There are three different types: some have one face (like a man's) and two wings; some have two faces (a man's and a lion's); some have four faces (a man's, a lion's, an ox's and an eagle's) and four wings. They have hands under their wings. They are concerned with the justice and might of God.
28. Ezek. 9:3; 10:1.
29. Isa. 6: 1–7.

30. Rev. 4:6–11.
31. 1 Pet. 1:12.
32. Ezek. 1:14.
33. Ezek. 1:8.
34. Ezek. 1:24.
35. Rev. 10:1.
36. Job 4:18–19.
37. Luke 9:26.
38. Col. 2:18.
39. Rev. 19:10.
40. Heb. 13:10; Zech. 1:8–10.
41. Ps. 34:7.
42. 1 Cor. 13:1.
43. Gen. 21:17; Judg. 6:22–23; Dan. 10:12; Matt. 1:20; 28:5; Luke 1:13, 30; 2:10; Acts 27:20.
44. Judg. 13:15–18.
45. Acts 12:5, 7.
46. Col. 2:18.
47. 2 Cor. 11:14.
48. Num. 22:23.
49. 2 Kings 6:17.
50. Ps. 103:20–21.
51. Isa. 6:2–3.
52. Isa. 6:1–3.
53. Isa. 28:2.
54. Ps. 139:7–10.
55. Matt. 10:29–30.
56. Ps. 139:2–4.
57. Isa. 63:7–9.
58. Jer. 3:19–20.
59. Isa. 40:25–26.

Chapter 1

The Great Disaster

There's one planet that the Mighty One seems to love more than all the rest. He always calls it His 'footstool',[1] and all of us angels agree it's quite the most beautiful of them all – the planet Earth. When He first made it, it was covered in crystals and precious stones – it was indescribably lovely.[2] It was easy to guess which of us would be given *that* one to look after. Only the highest of the Cherubim – the greatest and most beautiful angel of all – was good enough to look after planet Earth.

In those days there was someone even more highly honoured than Michael – Lucifer – the most extravagantly beautiful creature the Mighty One ever made. On state occasions he used to soar above the Mighty One's throne, spreading wide his enormous sparkling wings like a gigantic canopy. A wonderful sight! No wonder he was nicknamed Lucifer, Son of the Morning.[3] So no one was surprised when he was made Prince of the Earth, which is what he still is to this very day.

To be quite honest, I never trusted him. I thought he was too beautiful for his own good – and far too smooth.[4]

We used to watch him strutting about down there on the favoured planet, like an Earthling cockerel, and gradually his own magnificence went to his head. He began to think he was as big and powerful as the Mighty One Himself. Can you credit such arrogance?[5] A mere angel, with all our limitations! But his smooth talk took in lots of angels from all ranks and departments, and they followed him about like pet dogs. The Mighty One put up with his swaggering lies and silly antics for ages, but finally it was Lucifer's pride which undid him.

'Mine be the Kingdom, the power and the glory' – that was his rallying call when he demanded that his followers should worship him. The very idea! It was disgusting!

'Choose!' he would yell at us all. 'Choose which master to serve. Why let yourselves be ordered about like slaves? I'll give you freedom if you bow to me. Stick with me and I'll see you're all right.' More like 'all wrong'! That's what a lot of us thought, anyway. But one third of all angels were taken in completely and they chose Lucifer.[6] Bad day for Heaven, that was!

Of course, he and all his entourage had to be banished, and the great and powerful Michael himself was given the unpleasant job of hurling them out of the gates of Heaven.[7,8]

It nearly broke his heart, because he and Lucifer had been fellow Archangels – best friends – but we all knew Lucifer had to go, and all his followers with him. I saw them falling like lightning out of heaven.[9] It was a terrible sight! Down they went – twisting, squirming, spiralling down, totally unrepentant – and as they went they changed. Their angelic light changed to darkness, and the beauty of their faces became contorted by rage and hate. One third of all the angels are now known as demons[10] and, like the rest of us, they can never die,[11] but what's the point of living without the Mighty One?

I have to confess that I was curious enough to peep through my wing feathers at the Mighty One's face as He watched them all being thrown out, one after another. I thought He'd look angry, but no! Like I said, He's Love – and that's His problem. He looked even more heartbroken than Michael. I doubt if He's got over it yet. If only He hadn't been Love!

I think I'd better explain. Until that moment all angels had the power to choose whether we served the Mighty One or disobeyed Him.[12] Until Lucifer started puffing himself up, no angel had ever used that power of choice, but after that terrible occasion the Mighty One removed it from us – and from the Others. We can't choose to be bad and they can't choose to be good.[13] No creature is free unless they have the power of choice. It's the greatest gift of all – and Lucifer robbed angels of it.

Anyway, down they all fell to Lucifer's territory, and made their headquarters in Earth's atmosphere.[14] Stationed there, between Heaven and Earth, they can watch what goes on in either place and cause the maximum amount of havoc.

Now learn this fact – it's vital! Lucifer is Hate – just as the Mighty One is Love. He's behind all the trouble in the universe. He never does anything else but make nasty plans to balk and upset everything that the Mighty One wants to do. He doesn't have enough power to hurt the Mighty One Himself, so he goes for anyone who belongs to Him. Yes, he's a deadly enemy all right, and none of you will go far in your careers without clashing with one of his little boot-licking yes-men. And don't fall for the ridiculous Earthling error of thinking that they've all got sweet little horns, kid's hoofs and pretty little tails! They're all masters of disguise, so they sometimes do appear as animals,[15] but they get their best fun when they're allowed to live in the body and mind of a human.[16] The Earthling has to be willing to give them control, of course, but a surprising number of them do – probably because Lucifer's Lot offer them riches and power. The misery that Lucifer causes to Earthlings is indescribable. He hardly ever bothers to land on Earth himself. He controls humans and world affairs by a highly efficient and rigidly structured network of demons, whom he sends swarming all over the planet to put his evil plans into operation.[17]

Yes, you'll soon see how much easier life would be for us Holy Angels if it weren't for The Other Sort. There are more of us than there are of them, of course, and our Master is far more powerful, but they do cause us a lot of hassle! They know that the Mighty One has promised to banish the lot of them to the Lake of Fire soon.[18] They're making the most of their time, because it's rapidly running out.[19] Why the Mighty One doesn't just kick them into the Lake right away is another of the many things that we angels don't know, but we *do* know that He must have a reason. And anyway, we weren't created to understand, just to serve.

You should have seen what happened to Earth after that! Lucifer just didn't bother to look after it any more, and it soon ran to ruin – gas, steam and melted materials boiled and bubbled in a great seething, formless mess.[20] We thought the Mighty One would leave it like that as a lesson for

Lucifer. And, I must say, up here in Heaven things settled down very peacefully without him.

✱

Then suddenly one day the Mighty One amazed us all by announcing to a Full Assembly of Heaven that He intended to create an entirely new kind of being.

'We will call him Man,' He told us. 'And We will make him in Our own image.'[21]

There was a startled silence in Heaven while we tried to take in all the implications. First we felt awed. This new creature, if it were to be in the Mighty One's 'own image', would have to be an incredibly marvellous being. Then some of us began to feel a bit upset, and a senior Warrior Angel even dared to ask, 'Why create a new being, Most Glorious One?'

We all wanted to add, 'Weren't we enough for You? Haven't we served you well enough, said "Holy, Holy, Holy" loudly enough to please You?' But angels weren't created to argue, just to serve.

The Mighty One soothed us down gently, telling us what a great job we do, and stuff like that, but then He went on to say, 'I need to make a new creature because I am Love. Love cannot love in a vacuum. Love must receive love in return, and I didn't give angels the capacity to love. I will create mankind to love Me – to be the companions of My Heart.'

Flabbergasted, that's what the Seraphim were! After all, they spend all their time worshipping Him, yet here He was, saying He wanted *companions* for His heart. But worse was to follow. He told us this 'Man' creature was going to live on Lucifer's planet – where he still rules.[22] 'Surely,' we thought, 'it would be better to play safe and go for Mars or even the

Moon.' But all we could do was settle down to watch what would happen next.

First, the Mighty One had to re-create the Earth. He went to work on the molten mess while Lucifer jumped up and down screeching, 'You're invading my space! Not fair! You wait!' The Mighty One took no notice, but just went on shaping mountains, gouging out valleys and scooping ocean beds, to confine the flood-waters. He edged the sea with long, sandy beaches and scratched out the courses of rivers and streams. We heard Him laughing out loud in delight when He invented waterfalls, and let them trickle through His fingers. We watched Him flattening out bleak moors and wide deserts, forming lakes and then making mud pies to throw into the middle of them – calling them 'islands'. Then plants and trees began to grow, and soon He had forests, jungles and woodland, separated by stretches of grass and flowers.[23]

The colours! The sheer variety! It was fascinating to watch Him at work. How He enjoyed designing the intricacies of butterfly wings, and the complex world of the ants. He laughed over the waddling ducks and squealing little pigs; he was so happy. He *loves* creating. Rumour has it that when He finally gets rid of Lucifer He'll scrap Earth completely – and Heaven as well – and give Himself the pleasure of creating them all over again.[24]

Well, finally, when He'd finished making everything else, He created a Garden.[25] The like of that Garden has never been seen – before or since. What a place! Only the finest plants were allowed to flourish there, and great trees provided shade. Eden, that's what He called it.

'This is where my friends are going to live,' He told us. All we could say was, 'He must love this new being very much indeed to go to this much trouble for it.'

The Great Disaster

When the flowers and plants in the Garden had reached perfection, we sensed that the *great moment* had arrived at last. The atmosphere of anticipation in Heaven was positively electric.

You'll have to admit that we fully mature angels are extremely beautiful creatures (although I shouldn't say so myself). It would have been hard, even for the Mighty One Himself, to create something more magnificent than one of us. No wonder we were all agog – until at last we saw ...

Man!

A ridiculous, puny little thing with a pinky brown skin. He didn't glow with inner light, as we do. His body didn't look like flames of fire, constantly changing shape as he moved. He didn't glitter like sunshine on snow-capped mountains. He had no fur to keep him warm like Earth animals, no feathers like the birds to keep out the rain. He didn't even have any wings – just two flat feet to get about on and two little hands. He was so limited, so helpless! He didn't have four feet for speed or sharp teeth and claws for protection. He really was pathetic! Surely the Mighty One didn't want to be friends with an odd little creature like this! Was He teasing us?

But He wasn't. And after a while we did begin to realize that man, and then his wife, did have something that the animals and birds hadn't been given. Inside their odd little bodies humans have a spirit. We angels are all spirit, and nothing else. But man is made in the Mighty One's image, which means that he has three parts.[26] He has a body – the bit that's covered with skin. Then inside that he has a soul – the part of him that thinks and feels, his will and personality. In those two parts he is still like the animals – they have a body too, and many of them have a primitive kind of soul.

But man has one more part which puts him way beyond other Earth creatures – a spirit.[27] This is designed to communicate directly with the Mighty One – giving him a unique capacity to know Him, hear Him, talk to Him and, most important of all, to love Him.

By the way, it is that spirit part of an Earthling that Lucifer's Lot try to infiltrate. If they can live in the spirit of a man they can control his soul and his body and 'cock a snook' at the Almighty at the same time. You see, His Majesty designed that part of man as a place where His Spirit can live – providing the Earthling gives his permission.

✸

When the Mighty One had finally settled this man, and then his companion, in their own private paradise on Earth, we all sighed with relief. Perhaps we could relax now that He'd finished all that hard work, and maybe we could get a bit of peace for a millennium or two. Instead, our troubles had only just begun!

'My greatest gift of all to my new creation is the gift of choice,'[28] the Mighty One announced, just when we were all getting nice and comfortable.

'Choice!' We were horrified. Even ordinary, working-class angels like me could see the danger of that. 'Look what choice did for Lucifer's Lot!' we muttered. 'Surely man would be far better off without it.'

Gabriel and Michael hurried up to the Great Throne, making the usual 'Holy, Holy, Holy' sound like an urgent protest. The Mighty One was very nice to them, but He said sadly, 'I have to let them choose whether to love me or not.[29] Love can't be demanded. It isn't real love if there is no alternative. Love is only real if it's given voluntarily.'

A long and extremely uncomfortable silence hung over Heaven like a damp cloud. We all wanted to ask the same question, but only Gabriel dared – and his normally silvery voice sounded more like a croaky whisper:

'But suppose ... suppose ...' Gabriel was so distressed that his face was buried in his wings. 'But suppose ... some of those humans choose *not* to love You?'

The silence deepened as we all waited in agony for the Mighty One's answer. At last He sadly shook His head and said softly, 'Most of them will.'

After a while I dared to peep at Him through my wing feathers, and His face looked so desperately hurt. *That* was the moment when we began to realize just how vulnerable love was going to make Him.

Then He added, 'You angels will never understand this, but, you see, it would still be worth all the trouble and heartache if only one of these special ones chose spontaneously to love Me. That is how precious their love is to me.'

We comforted ourselves by thinking, 'How could they refuse His love? After all, look what He's given them!' Those two humans had everything: a lovely place to live; their health; physical beauty; good food; leisure; each other; and, most of all, they had the undivided attention of the Mighty One Himself. That was more than we angels had ever been given.

Every evening He would go down and *walk* with them, *Himself*, enjoying the flowers in their Garden, chatting over the day's events, laughing.[30] No covering of faces and saying 'Holy, Holy, Holy' for them! They could look right into His face and see the tenderness of His love for them. Surely they couldn't help but respond to love like that – or so we thought!

He only made one rule for them: they could have any-thing they wanted, except the fruit of one particular tree right in the middle of the Garden.[31] With so many others to choose from, we didn't think that would be a problem. But it was!

One terrible day a group of Watcher Angels rushed back into Heaven shouting, 'Beware – Lucifer! He's actually gone to Earth *himself*! He's in the Garden of Eden – dressed up as a reptile.'[32]

We threw down our harps, stopped singing 'Hallelujah' and ran to look out of the windows of Heaven. Sure enough, there he was, slithering along, large as life, and sweet-talk-ing the woman.

Some of the younger Messenger Angels clamoured to go down and warn her. 'Surely,' they protested, 'she ought to know how dangerous Lucifer is?'

The Warriors were straining at the leash too, vying with one another as to which one would slash the head off that serpent first.

But I've already told you, we are powerless up here to intervene in the affairs of men, unless they ask the Mighty One for help. All Eve had to do was say, 'Mighty One, give me wisdom – protect me,' and the entire history of the universe would have been quite different.

'The Mighty One can't let her listen to Lucifer!' wailed the younger angels. 'He must do something to stop this disaster!'

'*She has the right to choose*,' the great voice of Michael boomed across Heaven, silencing us all.

And Eve chose *not* to ask for our help – just like most of her descendants have done ever since. So we could do noth-ing to avert the approaching catastrophe. We had to stand still as we heard her say, 'We can eat any fruit we like except the fruit from that tree there, the one in the middle. If we even touch that fruit we'll die.'

Then to our disgust we heard Lucifer saying in that oily drawl of his, 'No, no, my dear, that's not true at all. You won't die. God just wants to keep you ignorant. He knows that if you eat fruit from that tree you will know the difference between right and wrong – like He does. It's not fair – He just doesn't want you to be free. You ought to rely on your own judgement, make your own decisions. God's just a tyrant – a fun-spoiler. You ought to look out for number one; be true to yourself; stand up for your rights; look out for your own interests; do it *your* way.' (Lucifer was always one for clichés, and he's been trotting that old stuff out ever since with boring regularity.) I suppose sin began with his own declaration of independence, so he tries to lure Earthlings to follow him.

We saw Eve take the first big bite, and then she gave some to her husband. It was a terrible moment! We were so upset for the Mighty One that we could do nothing but play dirges and requiems. For once I felt glad that we angels can't love, because when you love you can be wounded so painfully when the object of your love rejects you. It's better never to love at all.

We'll never forget the heartbreaking sound of the Mighty One's voice, calling to them that evening in the Garden:[33] 'Where are you, Adam?' The sound echoed around the whole Earth, and Heaven too, but there was no answer. Adam and Eve were hiding. Their spirits had died, you see. If Earthlings choose to reject the Mighty One's love and turn deliberately to selfishness, their spirits shrivel up and die inside them. They are separated from Him because He can never come close to disobedience – He's too holy, you see. His purity burns like fire and consumes anything impure which comes near to Him.

Well, they had to be shut out of their beautiful Garden home. Since they had eaten from the tree of life, they would have lived for ever without a spirit, which would have been unbearable. No lesser rank than the Cherubim themselves were sent down with flaming swords to eject them and guard the eastern end of the Garden so that no human could ever return there.[34] The Cherubim would rather have used their swords on Lucifer himself, naturally, but the Mighty One said the time wasn't right just then.

'One day,' He told Lucifer, 'a descendant of the woman will crush your head, even though He will be wounded in the process.' That thought has frightened Lucifer ever since.

We thought that that would be the end of it. The Mighty One's great plan seemed to have been destroyed before it had a chance to begin. But the Mighty One doesn't give up that easily. Love never gives up, I suppose. When the Mighty One makes a plan, He won't let it go. He knew just what He was doing. It was only the rest of us who were mystified.

✱

Now we're going to take a short break, because I want to show you something. Help yourself to some angel food,[35] commonly known on Earth as manna, and then follow me in a neat line, please … leaving your harps just where they are, if you don't mind!

When you're all ready, come over to this window, because you can get a very good view of Earth from here. Yes, I know it does look horribly dark and gloomy down there, but look closer. Do you see all those little lights dotted about in the darkness? Some are widely spaced but most are clustered together, sometimes quite densely. They are the spirits of those who love the Mighty One. When Earthlings reach out to the Mighty One and return His love, their spirits are reborn. Seen from up here, some of them blaze like giant beacons in the gloom, and others just look like a tiny, wobbling candle-flame. But a lighted spirit is a receptive spirit. They can communicate with the Mighty One and He with them. A part of Him lives in those Earthlings, so in a small way they become supernatural beings.[36]

When the Mighty One sees one of these little lights flickering dangerously, He usually despatches a Warrior to give them extra protection. Even then, you'll sometimes see the light go out completely.[37] We angels dread that, because of the way it twists the Mighty One's heart. It makes Lucifer's day, of course. He and his Lot work hard, thinking up fresh ways to smother those lights. As I've already said, it's all-out war on planet Earth, and don't forget it. It's dangerous down there, for Earthlings and for Holy Angels.

But we'd better get back to work. We've certainly got plenty to do!

*

So out of the Garden of Eden those first Earthlings went, and they soon discovered the full impact of their bad choice. The perfect world which had been specially made for them was now polluted. Weeds began to grow, smothering the beautiful flowers and strangling their crops. Some had thorns which scratched their limbs, and others stung their feet. Pests attacked their fruit trees, and locusts gobbled their meadow grass and vegetables. Even the animals weren't tame any more. We had to laugh when the Watchers described Eve's consternation when she went to stroke a cuddly old lion and discovered that lions had definitely turned nasty. If it hadn't been for a bit of smart work by her Guardians, that would have been the end of the human race!

It wasn't so funny when, in later generations, germs began to develop which attacked Earthling bodies and diseases crept up on them. Illness and pain were never part of the Almighty's plans.[38]

Well, the first man and woman had a large family, and humans began to colonize the Earth. The Mighty One *still* wanted them to be His friends, but most Earthlings loved themselves more than they loved Him – or anyone else, for that matter. Things went from bad to worse down there for many generations. They lied to each other; grabbed things that weren't theirs; cheated; exploited the weak and helpless; killed one another in frightful ways and were endlessly cruel.[39] And all because of that wretched gift of choice. Nearly all of them *chose* to put their own interests first. If doing that had made them happy, it wouldn't have been so hard to watch, but they were nothing but miserable! The Mighty One couldn't stand it, and in the end He devised His famous Ten Rules of Happiness for them.

'If you want to be happy,' he told His Earthlings, through a Lighted One called Moses, 'just keep these rules.

'I designed you to live in families, because children need to grow up feeling safe, with two parents to love and provide for them. Their security develops from this. So no sex outside marriage, because that destroys the family unit.[40]

'I want each family to have their own home and land. Your sense of peace will develop when you are safely surrounded by your own possessions. But you won't feel safe if others envy what you have, so no jealousy.[41] It leads to stealing, and stealing destroys peace and security, so no taking what is not yours.[42]

'Envy also leads to violence and even to killing, which is stealing someone else's life. This is a total enemy to happiness.[43]

'I want you to enjoy your relationships with other people, and trust is an important basis for this. So always speak the honest truth to each other, because dishonesty destroys relationships.[44]

'I want you to live long, full and satisfying lives. I don't want you to dread being lonely and forgotten in your old age. So don't push your old people out when you consider them to be past their usefulness. Honour and respect them. The same applies to you young people – honour your parents, or you'll have endless family rows.[45]

'Idols and images of make-believe gods are representions of Lucifer in disguise. That is his way of getting the worship he's always craved. If you worship him, you most certainly will not find happiness.[46] So don't bow down to man-made idols, even if they are supposed to look like me.

'Remember that my name is too big to be used as a mere expletive when you stub your toe, or as a cheap oath when you want to clinch a business deal.[47]

'I don't want you getting ill and stressed out through overwork, so take a day off every week. Stay at home with the family, enjoy the world I made for you, rest your body, and give your soul time to catch up with the week's experiences.[48] Laugh a little, think a bit, play music and show the family that you love them. But don't forget that I made you in three parts; you have a spirit as well as a soul and a body. You will only find complete happiness by communicating with Me. So on that day make time to worship Me, enjoy Me, listen to Me – revel in My company. Remember that if you put Me first in everything and make Me the centre of your life – the hub of your wheel – then everything else will function smoothly, in perfect balance.

'You'll keep all these rules effortlessly when you realize that the two most important things in life are to love Me with everything you've got and to love other people just as much as you love yourself.'[49]

You're all too newly created to realize why we angels feel so sad when we think about those ten rules. Down on Earth they call them the 'thou shalt nots' and curse the Mighty One for trying to spoil their fun. But *if only* they could all have even *tried* to keep those rules, life down there on Earth would have been so different! But Lucifer's Lot kept trotting out the same old clichés: 'You've got to look out for number one; be true to yourself; stand up for your rights; do your own thing...' And, of course, most Earthlings chose to listen, and the mess on Earth grew worse and worse.[50]

Now and again an isolated individual would respond to the Mighty One's love, and provided they were sorry for their failings, their spirits were lighted. Yet as time went by, things on Earth got so bad that there were very few of these lights left burning.

Then one day the Mighty One gathered all Heaven together round His throne and said, 'I'm going to let you into My secret. Humans are finding it hard to relate to me because they don't know what I'm like. They can't see a spirit, and most of them can only believe in what they can experience with their five senses. It's no good sending you lot down there to tell them what I'm like, because they get so terrified when they catch sight of you. So I've chosen a man called Abraham to show the rest of the Earthlings that I'm not some distant, frightening spirit, but someone who loves them and wants to help them live happily. By watching Abraham they will discover the benefits of friendship with me.'

To us angels it seemed like a very sensible plan, but we just hoped Lucifer didn't get to hear about it. 'Abraham will found a family,' the Mighty One continued, 'and he will teach his children and grandchildren to love and obey Me, so that family, too, will show the world that I care. Eventually they will form a nation, and I've chosen that nation to be My very own people. Not because I have favourites, but because I will use them as a demonstration model for the rest of the human race.'[51]

'But suppose this new nation chooses not to love Him?' whispered one small Messenger, who was hastily sat on by a nearby Cherub.

After the meeting we all stood around in groups, talking it over. Everyone knew that the little Messenger had put his wing feather right on the one flaw in the plan, but no one wanted to say so. It was easier to talk about smaller worries.

'Why choose Abraham? He's just an ordinary old man,' some of us asked Gabriel. 'What's so special about him anyway?'

'Nothing really,' Gabriel replied, 'except that he loves the Mighty One. That counts for everything, you see.'

Now, I've decided to use this old man and his family to explain to you young angels how the Mighty One uses us in His dealings with human beings. So sit still and listen hard.

Notes

1. Isa. 66:1.
2. Ezek. 28:13.
3. Isa. 14:12–15.
4. Ezek. 28:12–17.
5. Isa. 14:12–15.
6. Rev. 12:4.
7. 2 Pet. 2:4; Jude 6.
8. Rev. 12:7–9.
9. Luke 10:17–18.
10. Matt. 25:41.
11. Luke 20:35–36.
12. Dr Arnold G. Fruchtenbaum, *The Doctrine of Angels* (Ariel Ministries Press, PO Box 3723, Tustin, CA 92681, USA).
13. Fruchtenbaum, as above.
14. Eph. 2:2.
15. Gen. 3:1.
16. Luke 11:24–27.
17. Eph. 6:12.
18. Rev. 20:10.
19. Rev. 12:12.
20. Gen. 1:2.
21. Gen. 1:26.
22. John 12:31; 14:30; 16:11.
23. Job 38:4–7.
24. Rev. 21:1.
25. Gen. 2:8.
26. Thess. 5:23.
27. Zech. 12:1.
28. Gen. 2:16–17.
29. Matt. 23:37.

30. Gen. 3:8.
31. Gen. 2:16–17.
32. Gen. 3:1.
33. Gen. 3:9–10.
34. Gen. 3:24.
35. Ps. 78:25.
36. 1 John 4:12–13.
37. Heb. 6:4–6.
38. Gen. 1:3.
39. Gen. 6:5–6.
40. Exod. 20:14.
41. Exod. 20:17.
42. Exod. 20:13.
43. Exod. 20:13.
44. Exod. 20:16.
45. Exod. 20:12.
46. Exod. 20: 3–4.
47. Exod. 20:7.
48. Exod. 20:8–11.
49. Mark 12:29–31.
50. John 8:44.
51. Isa. 49:6; Ezek. 36:23b.

Chapter 2

Fire and Brimstone

A t first we simply could not understand why the
Mighty One should decide to found a nation by using
an elderly couple who'd never been able to have children. But you must remember that He always has a reason
for everything.

Abraham was living in a very luxurious house in Earth's
most prosperous city, and doing very well for himself in a
family business.[1] He looked a bit startled when a Messenger
Angel told him that God wanted him and Sarah to leave it all
– house, family, business, friends, everything – and set off to
a land they'd never even heard of.

But Abraham went. That's something else you'll have to
learn. Some Earthlings are so receptive to Heaven that they
seem 'tuned in' somehow. They can hear the smallest whisper from the Messenger Angels, while others only respond
to things in the ordinary world around them. If you're sent

to a Lighted One like that, it's a waste of time appearing to them or speaking audibly. You have to communicate your message through another, more susceptible Lighted One, or make them read the message in black and white in the Mighty One's book. I'll tell you more about that later. Abraham had one of the best developed 'spiritual receiving sets' any Earthling ever had. It was a delight for Messenger Angels to communicate with him.

When he and Sarah arrived in the land the Mighty One had designed for them, He told them that He meant to give it all to their descendants one day, but they still had no children.[2] They settled down quite well, considering the fact that they had swapped their comfortable house for a draughty old leather tent. But as the years went by and still no baby appeared, we did begin to wonder what the Mighty One was doing. They were growing older and more frail all the time. Then Gabriel explained:

'The Mighty One is teaching Abraham to trust. Love isn't love until it learns complete trust. And that is terribly hard for Earthlings, because they can't see how big and gloriously powerful the Mighty One is, as we angels can. Developing that trust is the toughest of all the Mighty One's jobs. It requires so much patience on His part that we angels marvel sometimes. Just when we think a Lighted One has really learnt to depend on Him completely, they suddenly have an unfortunate attack of *self*-confidence. And that *always* lands them in trouble.'

Abraham and his wife got so fed up waiting for God to send them a baby that they decided to help Him out a bit by using a surrogate mother. Sarah's Egyptian slave Hagar seemed like the obvious choice.[3]

Hagar was a strange girl – very passionate, sensual and

wild – and yet she was far more susceptible to the supernatural than her mistress was.

Well, Hagar fell pregnant straight away, and she started throwing her weight around and behaving so obnoxiously that she and her mistress quarrelled violently, and Hagar stormed off in a rage. The most painful wars on Earth are fought in families, not on military battlefields. Remember that.

Well, that stupid girl tried to run home to Egypt, not realizing that she'd have to cross a desert, where no one could survive unless they knew what they were doing. We could see the kind of terrain she was heading into, and her Guardian shot into the Mighty One's presence, wringing his hands.

'Your Mightiness, please give permission for an intervention, or she'll die of thirst!'[4] The Mighty One reacted in a most unusual manner – He beckoned to Michael. He is so immensely powerful that he is often known on Earth as 'the Angel of the Lord', and in fact he is often mistaken for the Mighty One Himself when he appears.[5]

'She carries the son of My friend, and he has asked me to protect her,' said the Mighty One, and then He added, 'and she herself is precious to me.' So off went Michael in his full glory, and I tell you, when he goes to Earth his radiance is so intense that the whole area is illuminated.[6] The poor girl didn't know what had hit her! Strange, really, that the Mighty One should send such a grand angel to protect an Earthling who was considered as less than nothing by her master. She was a woman, an Egyptian and a slave. On Earth you couldn't get lower than that! At that time a slave could be used like a dog – abused, starved, killed – and no one would raise an eyebrow. Down there, that girl was a worthless nothing, but to the Mighty One she was 'precious'.

That's something you are going to have to learn – the difference between the values of Heaven and Earth.[7] They see things totally differently.

By this time Hagar had realized the danger she was in and the sheer impossibility of reaching Egypt alive. She'd discovered a little wadi, and had collapsed in the scanty shade of some boulders. She was in a terrible state of distress by this time, knowing that if she went on she would die and that going back would also mean death. Runaway slaves were always killed as a deterrent to others. (I can see you're finding that hard to believe. I'm sad to say that you've got a lot to learn yet about Earthlings. Their cruelty towards one another never ceases to stagger us angels.)

Poor Hagar was huddled by that trickle of muddy water, sobbing like a child, feeling that no one loved her or cared where she was. If only she could have seen all the activity that was going on in Heaven on her behalf[8] or the look of love and compassion on the Mighty One's face as He despatched Michael to help her. Lighted Ones never seem to realize how important they actually are!

Because she was so busy crying, with her face hidden in her hands, she missed the first impact of Michael's radiance, but no Earthling could have failed to notice his voice! It sounds like a thunder-clap, right over head![9] If she'd been more like her mistress Sarah, she'd have said it *was* thunder, but for all her faults, she was a very susceptible Earthling indeed.

'What are you doing here, Hagar?' Michael boomed.

'I'm running away,' she managed to gasp, white as lamb's wool by this time.

'Go back and be a good slave to your mistress. Your distress has been noted in Heaven, and you will have more descendants than anyone can ever count. Your son will inherit your temperament and he, too, will be as wild as an untamed mountain donkey, pitting himself against the rest of the human race. But he will survive, and so will you, for the Lord God of Heaven Himself is with you.'

As I've already told you, humans often think Michael is the Mighty One Himself, and Hagar certainly did. For hours she just sat there, rocking back and forth muttering, 'He saw me, He knew I was crying, He knows my name.' You'll soon discover how wonderful it is for us angels when we see it dawning on Earthlings that they are loved and valued highly by the Mighty One. Sadly, very few Lighted Ones ever realize it fully. When they do, as Hagar did by that wadi, something incredible happens inside them. The knowledge that they are loved to the uttermost seems to set them free, gives them the power to live by a totally new value system, and nothing else that happens to them on Earth can ever bring them down.[10] At a moment like that we all have a party!

Hagar christened that little wadi 'The Well of the Living God Who Sees Me'. Then she squared her shoulders, thrust out her little chin and marched back home. When she told her master that she'd seen the Mighty One Himself, he spared her life, because he believed her (but I doubt if her mistress did!). A few months later Ishmael was born; and right from birth he was an awkward, contrary boy, just as Michael had said he would be. But Hagar loved him. If the Mighty One had not invented mother love, the human race would certainly not have survived. If Hagar hadn't had another encounter with Michael later in her life, she wouldn't have survived either,[11] but there isn't enough time to tell you that story now.

✱

Abraham and Sarah had so much hassle and grief[12] from Hagar and her son over the next few years, but it was all their own fault. You know, for us angels, one of the most frustrating things is knowing the lovely plans that the Mighty One has all ready and waiting for His Lighted Ones, and then seeing them ruining them, all because they just won't wait.

When the Mighty One finally knew the time was right to send a son to Abraham,[13] there wasn't a single angel in Heaven He considered important enough to announce the news to this Earthling, who had become His friend. So He decided to pay Abraham a visit in person. He does do that occasionally, with some people who are very close to Him, like Adam and Eve, Enoch and Moses.

He took two senior angels with Him, and all three of them were disguised as young men.

Abraham, sitting in the shade of some huge oak trees during the hottest part of the day, was astonished to see three travellers walking towards him. No one journeyed during siesta time – not even mad dogs – but he was the soul of hospitality, so he scrambled hastily to his feet and invited them all to a meal. Sarah was none too pleased to be shaken out of a deep sleep – women of her age like a good snooze at midday. She was even less pleased to be told to dash off to the camp kitchen and start cooking a real slap-up meal at that unheard-of hour of the day. But she and Hagar soon had an excellent spread laid out – cream, milk, freshly roasted meat, oat-cakes and a new batch of bread. Abraham served his guests himself, under the shady oak trees near his tent. Angels don't usually eat Earth food, but this was a very special occasion, and they gave an excellent impersonation of Earthlings enjoying themselves.

As he served the meal, Abraham kept giving the three of them very odd looks. You see, every evening he always spent time sitting alone under the stars talking with the Mighty One – friend to friend. He recognized the voice that he'd heard so many times before. The more time an Earthling spends with the Mighty One, the easier it is for him to recognize the Mighty One's voice when he hears it audibly. He was obviously beginning to realize that these visitors weren't just men. So the Mighty One decided that it was best to end the charade, and He came straight to the point.

'In nine months' time your wife will have a son,' He said. Abraham stood very still; he'd waited for this moment for the best part of a hundred years. But Sarah, behind the curtain in the kitchen, burst out laughing. Like I said, she didn't feel easy with the supernatural – and the poor old soul was 90, after all! A few months later she was sorry that she'd laughed!

The Mighty One had another reason for that visit to Abraham, so after the meal, in the cool of the evening, all four of them went for a stroll to the cliff which overlooked the great, wide plains. There they stood on the very edge, side by side, watching the evening shadows lengthening on the grassland far below. In the distance the smoke of two great cities curled upwards into the sky.

'Sodom and Gomorrah,' sighed the Mighty One. 'My Watchers keep bringing me so much bad news about those two cities – terrible accusations of perversion and bizarre sex – depravity of all kinds.'

'Oh dear,' said Abraham. 'My nephew Lot lives in Sodom.'

The Mighty One nodded to His two bodyguards, and they set off at once over the cliff-face, leaping fearlessly down the steep goat-path which zig-zagged the precipice.

'I may have to destroy those cities,' continued the Mighty One sadly. 'I can't let them contaminate the rest of the world. Depravity spreads like a plague, and the whole human race will be in danger.'

Abraham was upset. Lot was *family*.[14] But he knew the best way of helping him. Now here's another very important lesson coming up. The Mighty One has given Earthlings a massively powerful weapon, which they can use any time they like.[15] It's called prayer. If only they would realize just how much power it puts at their disposal! Lucifer loathes prayer, because it defeats him every time.

The prayer missiles that Earthlings launch towards Heaven have to pass through the atmosphere first, which, of course, is the territory of the Prince of the Powers of the Air,[16] so they come under heavy enemy attack.[17] In fact, none of them would ever get through if it weren't for the mighty Warrior Angels who constantly patrol the sky, watching out for the launch of even the most feeble little prayer rocket, and they'll hastily summon reinforcements when a group of Lighted Ones decide to go for a mass launch. Prayer is the ammunition that we angels use against Lucifer's Lot all the time. As soon as a missile arrives in Heaven and is noted by the Mighty One, we are allowed to fire it right back at the enemy. Without those prayers we can't attack the enemy at all; we depend entirely on prayer. If only Earthlings could grasp that, they'd realize that by spending one minute in prayer they can achieve more than if they worked for a year! You'll find that the Others will do anything whatsoever to discourage an Earthling from praying: cause distractions; thought-plant temptations or doubts; tell him to find something more important to do! But you'll also notice that when humans begin to pray, they are instantly surrounded by angels who spread out their wings to form a protective wall all round them.[18]

Anyway, Abraham *knew* how important prayer is, so he began to plead for his nephew's city.

'Surely You won't kill hundreds of innocent people, just for the sake of a few bad ones! Suppose there were 50 good, honest citizens – you'd spare the city to save them, wouldn't you? You're the Judge of all the universe, aren't you? So surely you must act fairly.'

'All right,' smiled the Mighty One. 'If my angels find 50 good people, I'll spare the rest.'

Abraham shuffled his feet a bit, and then plucked up his courage again.

'Suppose they only find 45?'

'That would still be all right,' was the reply; and so it went on all evening. (Don't start thinking you could ever talk to the Mighty One like that! Intimacy is reserved for His Lighted Ones. Angels weren't created to be intimate, just to serve.)

Abraham slowly worked down from 45 to 10, and then, as the awful truth gradually dawned on him, he finally whispered, 'There aren't any innocent people in Sodom and Gomorrah at all, are there?'

The Mighty One nodded. 'You go home,' He said, 'and whatever you do, don't look down into the plain until this horrible business is all over.'

Fire and Brimstone

Meanwhile the two angels were arriving at the city gates of Sodom, just as they were about to be locked for the night. Lot was on the city council, so he was sitting in committee right by the gates. As soon as he saw the two good-looking young men walking into that vice-infested dump, he realized that they were in great danger from the gay men of Sodom.

'Gentlemen,' he said, quickly scrambling to his feet, 'you are most welcome to come to my humble little home for the night.'

'It's all right, sir,' they answered. 'We can sleep in the street.'

Lot looked horrified. 'Not in Sodom, you can't,' he said in a shocked whisper, and he hustled them through the crowded marketplace and down the narrow streets. All around them they were conscious of eyes – greedy, lustful eyes – spying on them from keyholes, cracks in the doors, broken shutters and dark alleyways. They told us all, later, that an evil atmosphere covered the place like thick storm clouds.

Then the whispers and sniggers began.

'Quick!' said Lot. 'There's not a moment to lose,' and he pulled them in through his front door and slid the bolt firmly across. 'Just in time!' he gasped, as they heard the footsteps padding towards the house from all directions. 'Good-looking young men like you shouldn't come near a place like Sodom,' panted Lot. 'You'll drive them mad with desire. I really don't know if I can hold them off for long.'

The angels themselves weren't afraid, of course, because angels can't be hurt by Earthlings, but as we watched we felt furious on their behalf, as we saw every man in the city hurrying to surround Lot's house. You'll discover just how tough we find it when we have to go with our Lighted Ones into places where a lot of demons are concentrated. The smell of evil is frightful and, unlike our Earthling charges, we can actually *see* the fierce faces of our opponents leering at us – and hear their insulting threats.

'Bring them out, Lot, you spoilsport,' screamed the crowd, as stones rattled against the shutters and fists banged on the front door. Lot ran about the house wringing his hands.

'Mass rape,' he kept muttering, 'and they're visitors in my house! Whatever would Uncle Abraham say?'

Just then the pounding on the front door grew louder, as the men began to hurl themselves against it in a frenzy.

'They'll be in at any minute!' wailed Lot. He was an exceedingly silly little man – anyway, that's what we angels thought. Then he had an idea – a pathetic idea, but it made him feel better. Squeezing himself out of the door, and closing it firmly behind him, he faced the seething crowd in the street.

'Look, common courtesy won't let me give you these young men, but you could have my two daughters instead – do what you like with them!' A howl of derision greeted him. Those men weren't interested in young girls!

'You self-righteous little foreigner!' they yelled. 'Stop telling us what to do, or we'll have you too!'

Lot squealed with horror, and if the two angels hadn't grabbed him and pulled him back into the house, he would have been gobbled up by that lecherous gang of gays.

With one cool wave of their hands the angels struck the whole lot of them blind. We can do that when the need arises, or we can put a temporary screen round an Earthling so that he is invisible to his enemies.

How we laughed as we watched those Sodomites groping about, falling over each other and banging their heads against walls and doorposts! Eventually they all wandered off, howling with rage and fear, and the two angels locked the front door firmly once again.

Then they turned to Lot and his trembling family.

'We've come to get you all out of this city,' they said coolly, 'because tomorrow the Angels of Judgement are coming to destroy both Sodom and Gomorrah.'

'Oh my!' squeaked Lot. 'I don't think we could leave. This is our home, you see. My wife likes city life and my daughters hope to get married – sometime, anyway.'

All night long that stupid little man made excuses, even going so far as to suggest that the angels were joking.

'God won't destroy all these people,' he protested. 'He's supposed to be a God of Love, isn't He?' Earthlings find it hard enough to believe in nice angels, but when it comes to the Angels of Judgement ... well, they reject the very idea! These angels don't like their job at all, but sometimes they do have to be sent down to mete out punishment.[19] Fortunately, they're not sent very often, but when they are, their visits cause such an impact that they always make headlines in the history books. Their leader, the Angel of Death, once killed 185,000 soldiers who were attacking the Mighty One's people.[20] He finished them all off in one night and left the corpses strewn all over the ground by first light – a very messy business, that's what it was! Another time he killed 70,000 Jews in three days, and he would have wiped out the entire population of Jerusalem if King David hadn't sent up a huge prayer rocket.[21] Oh yes, the Angel of Death is grim – very grim indeed.

As dawn was breaking, the patience of those two angels in Sodom finally snapped.

'Quick!' they ordered, 'we're taking you *now*.' They told us later that they wished they could have dragged that ridiculous little man out by his hair, but unfortunately he was bald!

Down the street went the odd-looking little group, just as the city gates opened at dawn. Mrs Lot was carrying so many bags and bundles that she could hardly waddle, and Lot looked even fatter than usual because of all the money bags he was hiding under his robe.

'Hurry!' urged the Guardians. 'The Angels of Judgement will soon be here.'

'Superstition!' muttered Mrs Lot. 'If my friends could only see me now, how they'd laugh at this silliness.' She was in her element in that city. The two girls weren't much better, but they liked the look of the angels and they giggled and preened themselves so much that they were incapable of hurrying. When we assume human form we nearly always appear to them as 'perfect specimens' – very tall and handsome, with wonderfully developed muscles. So perhaps it was no wonder that those two girls were somewhat distracted.

'Come *on!*' shouted their Guardians, who could already see the Angels of Judgement waiting overhead.

All day they urged the family along the main camel route through the plain, the humans panting, puffing and protesting all the way. By the time they saw a small village in the distance, at the far end of the plain, the sky already looked yellow and sinister, and a hot, evil-smelling wind scorched their faces.

'I'm frightened!' wailed one of the girls. 'Perhaps something bad really is going to happen.' Just then they heard a weird, unearthly, rumbling sound. At first it came from the far distance but, as they listened, it grew nearer and louder by the second.

'Don't just stand there!' shouted the exasperated angels. 'Make for the village – fast. *And don't look back!*'

Lot tucked up his robes and ran with quite remarkable speed for someone with his enormous girth, and the girls pattered after him, screeching hysterically. But Mrs Lot stopped and peered back over her shoulder. The sky over Sodom and Gomorrah was black with acrid smoke, the rumble had become a terrifying roar and even the ground under their feet was shaking now.

Lot reached the village gates first; they were shut fast, while the inhabitants peered nervously through cracks and knot-holes. They did not intend to welcome any strangers. So the angels pulled open the gates, bursting the iron bolts with perfect ease, and bundled Lot and his daughters inside.

'Come on!' they yelled back into the gathering gloom, as they stood holding the gates open. But Mrs Lot, still clutching her precious belongings, stood stiff and petrified, too afraid to move. At that moment burning sulphur began to pour down from the skies, raining down on the plain and sending a huge tidal wave of molten lava crashing towards them. Mrs Lot never moved again. They found her several days later, covered with dust and encrusted with salty chemicals. She stood stiff and straight, still gazing back at her beloved city, her bags clutched in her lifeless hands. How those Earthlings do hang on to life! If only they could realize that their time down there is so brief in comparison with the eternity they'll enjoy up here with us.[22] Their time down there seems to angels no longer than the blink of a human eye. If only they could see their lives from our angle, little things wouldn't worry them so much.

Later in the morning of the disaster Abraham came back to the cliff edge where he had stood next to the Almighty and pleaded for the cities. Black smoke rose from the plain, and he wept when he saw the terrible devastation.

'Was my nephew not righteous enough to be spared?' he asked.

'No, he was not,' was the gentle reply of the Messenger Angel beside him, 'but the Mighty One spared him and his children because of your prayers.'

In spite of all that the Mighty One had done for them, Lot and his daughters never trusted Him, and their story has an end which is far too nasty for your newly created ears.[23]

✻

Just nine months to the day since the Mighty One and his angels came for lunch, Sarah safely gave birth to a baby boy.[24] His birth, to such ancient parents, was a huge joke all round the district, and caused so much amusement that they called him Isaac, which means 'Laughter', and he grew up with a marvellous sense of humour to match.

Now I need to tell you something vitally important which will help you to understand the Lighted Ones who'll be put in your care.

The trouble with most of them, at least as far as we angels can see, is that they just don't know when they're onto a good thing. They have the Almighty ready and waiting to supply everything that matters down there on Earth – love, fulfilment, knowing that they're special and will never die – not to mention little things like clothes and food![25] For humans who are willing to give Him a free hand in their lives, He can even take the *bad* things which all humans experience and turn them round to their advantage.[26] Yet the silly creatures constantly look to other Earthlings to give them the things they need, rather than going directly to the Mighty One. He created them with a built-in need for love, hoping that they'd fill that void with His love.[27]

Even the Lighted Ones are desperate to build organizations and businesses; to create beautiful homes; to change the world; to make piles of money – just to make themselves feel that they're worth something. I suppose they all know how short their lives on Earth really are, and they can't stand the idea of just being an insignificant dot on their globe, so they try to make themselves indispensable and strive to achieve things in order to feel important. And when they've done it, they're so exhausted with the effort that they die! And then what? They can't bring a speck of gold up here with them.[28] We don't need any more – we just use it for covering roads.[29] We just have to laugh at those Earthlings, otherwise we'd cry (except, of course, that there's no crying here in Heaven).[30]

*

Well, the Mighty One wanted His friend Abraham to be different because, like I said, He wanted to use him as a role-model for all human beings. And for all those years, while he waited for Isaac, Abraham relied on the Mighty One quite well – most of the time. Then, when he'd finally got the son he'd waited for, things changed almost overnight. Instead of the Almighty being the centre of Abraham's universe and the one he looked to for all his happiness and fulfilment, he shifted his devotion to his baby son. He was besotted – he couldn't take his eyes off the little fellow.

'I don't have to worry about a thing, now that I have a son,' he'd croon over the cot. 'When you grow up, you'll see that I'm all right, won't you? If bandits start pinching my sheep, you'll soon see 'em off. And when I get too old to do much, you'll take care of all the herds and keep the servants in order. I haven't lived for nothing now that I've got a son to carry on my name, and I'll never be a lonely old man now that I've got you. You'll always be there for me, won't you, son?'

Really! Some of these Earthlings would make us angels feel sick, if angels *could* feel sick! It was such an insult to the Mighty One, who had always made sure that he was all right, who had protected him and supplied him with the best of everything – and wasn't it enough to be called the Almighty's friend? That should have made him feel important, surely? So why was he suddenly putting all his trust in a baby who could do nothing but puke up his milk?

When Lighted Ones start behaving like that, the Mighty One gets restless. And don't go thinking that He's just being petty and jealous – He can see the danger they're in. How was Abraham going to feel if that son of his said 'Nuts to you!' as soon as he was grown up, or took himself off to the city lights, like his uncle Lot before him? Or suppose he caught a fever and died; or he could easily have been wiped out by his jealous half-brother Ishmael, son of Hagar. Human love is so unpredictable, and it can't last past death. It's not that the Mighty One is against them loving each other – of course He's not – but they're only safe if He comes first and the other loves fall in line behind.[31]

We could see that Abraham was in danger of getting his love for Isaac right out of proportion, but we were totally unprepared for what happened when the boy reached his early teens.

Notes

1. Gen. 12:1.
2. Gen. 15:18.
3. Gen. 16:1–2.
4. Job 33:23–24.
5. There are certain places in the Old Testament which refer to 'the Angel of the LORD'. Commentators disagree over his identity. Some say he was a particularly powerful angel.Others hold that these verses refer to God Himself or the Second Person of the Trinity appearing on Earth before the incarnation. Others say that he was a leading but unnamed angel; some think this was the Archangel Michael or Gabriel. For the sake of simplicity in this book, I have decided to stay with the last opinion.
6. Ezek. 1:4–5.
7. Mark 9:34–35.
8. Dan. 10:12–14.
9. Ezek. 1:24.
10. Rom. 8:35–37.
11. Gen. 21:9–21.
12. Gen. 16:45 and 21:9–10.
13. Gen. 18:10.
14. Gen. 18:20–33.
15. Neh. 1:4.
16. Eph. 2:2.
17. It is hard to find chapter and verse for this paragraph, but the concept of prayer as warfare is obvious from passages such as Eph. 6:10–18.
18. 'God's angel sets up a circle of protection around us while we pray' (Ps. 34:7, *The Message*).
19. Rev. 9:15–21; 15:1, 6–8; 16:1–21.

20. 2 Kings 19:35.
21. 1 Chron. 21:14.
22. Ps. 103:14–17.
23. Gen. 19:30–38.
24. Gen. 21:1–3.
25. Matt. 6:25–26.
26. Rom. 8:28.
27. Isa. 30:18.
28. Ps. 49:16–19.
29. Rev. 21:21.
30. Rev. 21:4.
31. Luke 14:26.

Chapter 3

The Family that Shocked Heaven

One evening the Mighty One leant down from Heaven in Abraham's direction and called his name.[1] The old man was a bit startled – he hadn't heard the Mighty One's voice since the boy had been born. Somehow he'd got out of the habit of sitting under the stars of an evening, chatting to his Best Friend. He'd rather be telling a bedtime story to that son of his.

What we heard the Mighty One say to Abraham sent shockwaves rippling to the farthest corners of Heaven.

'Take that boy of yours, the one you love so much, and go with him to that mountain you can see in the far distance. When you get there, build a table out of stones, cut his throat and then burn his body as a sacrifice to Me.'

We simply couldn't believe our ears – the silence in Heaven was profound. It was so unlike Him. Human sacrifice was something He could not abide. In fact, He would always despatch the Angels of Death to wreak judgement on any community which offered their children to Lucifer.

Our blood ran cold – well, it would have done if angels *had* blood. But Abraham never argued, and first thing next morning he was up and off.

That is the kind of complete obedience and trust that the Mighty One looks for in a Lighted One, but it's very rare – generally humans hate that word 'obedience' like poison. When will they learn that the Almighty never asks them to do anything which is not for their highest good and greatest happiness? When He tells angels to do something it isn't for our benefit; we were created to serve. But men weren't – they were created to be loved. Yet they still refuse to obey because they want to be in control of their own lives, even though they must know that they don't have the power to see into the future, or to know what other people are going to do. So how can they possibly know what's best for them?[2] Trying to 'do their own thing' makes them so anxious and fearful, yet if they could only trust the Mighty One they would be as carefree and happy as little Earthling children, playing on a warm sunny seashore.

As we watched that old man doggedly walking towards Mount Moriah, we knew he must really love the Mighty One; but did he love Him as much as he loved his son? We had to wait and see. There were others watching them, too. Lucifer gave the pair his full attention, and his spies were stationed behind every rock. As those two plodded up the mountain-side, hauling a load of sticks and a portable brazier, we angels were getting very jumpy. We could see something that Isaac hadn't noticed – the long, sharp-bladed knife that his father had hidden inside his tunic. The atmosphere in Heaven that day was so tense that not even the Seraphim could bring themselves to play a single note, and the Mighty One's face was firmly set.

All Heaven watched as they collected the stones and built the altar. We wondered when the Mighty One was going to step in and stop this farce. He was really pushing His friend to the limit.

Isaac was a lovely lad, full of laughter, and he'd never been hurt in his life. He looked a bit surprised as his father tied him up, but he didn't struggle. You see, he had that kind of trusting love for his father that the Mighty One was looking for in Abraham; the kind which says, 'I know you'll only ever do what's best for me, and you're wise enough to *know* what is best.'

The blade of the knife glinted in the sunshine, and suddenly a sigh of relief spread all over Heaven. The Mighty One nodded in the direction of the Messenger Angel who was standing ready beside him. Off he went instantly – he didn't even wait to reach Earth before he shouted '*Stop!*' as he darted downwards. 'Don't hurt the boy!' he added as he landed, invisible beside that ghastly stone table. 'Look, there's an old ram tangled up in the bushes over there. Use him instead.'

Abraham mopped his forehead, and up here the choirs began to sing again. Later that night, when the stars came out, the father and son were still sitting at the top of that mountain, close together, not talking much. Just being close to each other was all that mattered, and it was then that the Mighty One spoke to them directly. No angelic go-between this time.

'See those stars,' He said. 'No one can count them but Me, and I'm going to give you as many descendants as those stars, and every nation in the world will be blessed because of you.' You see, the Mighty One just can't do enough for those who really love and obey Him.

'Remember, if your descendants put me first in everything,' He continued, 'then I'll always put *them* first too, and endless blessings will be theirs. That's a bargain.'

✤

Now you may be sitting there thinking, 'That story ended happily for everyone but the ram.' Well, there's something you young angels are going to have to understand. Remember me telling you about those first humans, Adam and Eve? Well, they had a son called Abel. He was a Lighted One, and loved the Mighty One so much that he wanted to give Him a present. He didn't have anything much to give, except a pet lamb that he'd tamed and come to love.[3] He knew he couldn't hand the lamb up to Heaven, so the only way of offering it was through the flames of fire as they burnt up the lamb's body. The Almighty was very touched, and giving gifts by fire like that became a recognized way to please Him. Later men began to place their hand on the animal's head as it died and pictured all their silly mistakes and the nasty, mean, cruel things they'd done passing into the animal – who then died in their place.[4] As the fire burnt the body of the lamb the flames purified the man's spirit, making it possible for him to look into the Mighty One's face without embarrassment. For a while animal sacrifices became a vital part of the relationship between the Mighty One and His Lighted Ones.

Now I'm going to tell you about another very important aspect of our work, so pay close attention – especially you lot whispering in the back row!

When Isaac was 40 Abraham sent his senior slave Eliezer on a dangerous journey hundreds of miles long, in search of a bride for his son.[5] The old man didn't want him marrying one of the local girls who hadn't been brought up to know the Mighty One; his bride must be a Lighted One.

'Go to my brother,' he told Eliezer, 'and see if he's got any nice daughters about the right age.' Poor Eliezer was horrified!

'How will I ever find your brother, Master?' he asked incredulously. 'You haven't had word from him for years, and even if he has a daughter, she's not likely to risk coming back with a strange man to marry someone she's never even met!'

'Don't worry,' Abraham replied cheerfully, 'God will send His angel to guide you.' And that was that as far as Abraham was concerned, and quite right too. Whenever Lighted Ones are sent out on special assignments for the Mighty One, as well as their usual Guardian, they are also given a special angel to guide them. Their official instructions are to take charge of the Lighted One and to accompany, defend and preserve them.[6] Afterwards, of course, the Lighted One will recount the amazing story of his adventures, describing how he found himself 'at the exact spot at just the right time to meet the one and only person who could help him.' All his listeners say, 'What an incredible coincidence!' What they don't realize is just how hard that invisible Angel Guide had to work to bring all the little details together so precisely!

Typically, Eliezer was *astounded* when Rebekah, his master's niece, 'just happened' to be at some obscure well at precisely the moment when he and his camel train arrived. So Isaac soon had a wife. We angels love romance – although, of course, we weren't created to marry, just to serve. We don't have close relationships with each other –

we all get on equally well.[7] Sometimes I can't help thinking how much better it would have been if the Mighty One had made Earthlings function like that too! But, like I say, He always has a reason.

While I'm on the subject of marriage, there is something rather nasty that I feel you ought to know. While Holy Angels don't marry, Fallen Angels can have sex with Earthling women. Long before the days of Abraham, Lucifer had what he thought was a brilliant idea – a plan to infiltrate the human race and pollute it completely. He sent a group of his most powerful demons down to Earth, disguised as handsome young men.[8] They courted the prettiest girls they could find and finally mated with them. Lucifer's Lot can actually create life, as well as imitating the Mighty One's miracles.[9] The progeny from those unions were magnificent – in fact they were giants, with supernatural strength and psychic powers. Legends are still told about their achievements to this day. But they were totally evil, and the Mighty One was so angry that He sent a great flood which drowned nearly everyone on Earth – except for a Lighted One called Noah and his family.[10] So Lucifer was balked that time, but you'll still find perverted sex wherever Lucifer is worshipped, and you can be sure his demons are heavily involved!

✸

Well, Isaac and Rebekah were married and, after a long wait, twin sons arrived.[11] We angels secretly feel that Isaac was a shocking father. He adored one of his boys and he was always picking on the other, who never seemed able to do anything right. Because one was born holding onto the other's ankle, they were officially born simultaneously, so he should have

The Family that Shocked Heaven

asked the Almighty which boy should be classed as the eldest son and heir. But dear old Isaac was so easy-going that he never got round to asking the Mighty One's advice about anything important. He just assumed that his favourite would also be the Almighty's choice.

But only one of those boys was a Lighted One, and it wasn't Esau, the father's favourite. He couldn't care less about the Mighty One and was totally unsusceptible to the supernatural world. He lived for the pleasure of the moment. He was all body – not much soul and no spirit at all. Jacob was totally different. We noticed his spirit ignite with love for the Almighty while he was scarcely more than a baby. His love blazed bright as a furnace, but it was a hungry kind of a love – never satisfied. He used to sit next to his grandfather Abraham, looking up at the stars and listening to the old man talking about his friendship with the Mighty One and the pact they had made together.

'Why couldn't I be the one to be chosen by God to be the father of His people?' Jacob used to ask himself. 'Why should Esau inherit the blessing, when he doesn't even *want* to be blessed by God – or to be loved by Him either?'

As he grew up, his love for the Mighty One deepened, but he found trusting God much harder and, like I've said, the two must go together. Instead of going to the Mighty One directly and telling Him how much he wanted that blessing and asking for help, Jacob tried to work the problem out by himself. If *only* he'd prayed, the Mighty One would have acted instantly. He always answers the prayers of his Lighted Ones; perhaps not in the way they expect, but He never, ever ignores their prayers. If only those poor, bewildered little creatures would learn that, but Lucifer's agents are always telling them they're strong and clever enough to look after themselves. Ridiculous! But I suppose Lucifer *has* to stop Lighted Ones trusting the Mighty One completely, because he knows only too well that if they did, there would be no limit to their power.

Not only did Jacob find trusting the Mighty One hard, but he was also crooked. It was almost as if he was afraid that others would disapprove of the real Jacob behind the mask he always seemed to wear. We angels thought it was because his father never made a fuss of him and instead called him a wimp and said things like, 'Why can't you be a sportsman or a hunter, like your brother Esau?'

When you become Guardian Angels you'll soon find how exasperated we get with talk like that. Young Earthlings can be destroyed by their own well-meaning parents, damaged not so much by the things that are *done* to them as by the things that are *said* to them. And watch out for phrases like, 'You ought to have been a boy', 'You were an accident', 'You're always so clumsy' or 'I won't love you if you do that again.' Ugh! Verbal spears like that[12] wound and scar the souls of Earthling children, causing them to grow up with distorted ideas about themselves which are fixed for life – unless they turn to the Mighty One for healing. And He *can* heal them, of course, but Lucifer's Lot love to tell them otherwise.

You're probably wondering why the Guardians don't prevent all those destructive words – and the violence and sexual abuse too. Well, we can't, for the same old reason – that wretched gift of choice. The adults who hurt them have the freedom to choose either to hurt and abuse or to build and encourage. We can only intervene if the child cries to the Mighty One for help,[13] or if another Earthling prays for them. Otherwise all we can do is try to comfort the child afterwards, as best we can.

Of course, Lucifer's Lot were attacking Jacob too. 'God doesn't love you – you're not good enough,' they'd whisper, and then cackle gleefully as they watched the way their barbs twisted Jacob up in knots because he'd never felt 'good enough' to earn his father's love.

But nothing was going to stop Jacob from getting that inheritance, and he managed it too, first by cheating his brother into promising him all the financial rights of the eldest son; then by dressing up as his brother and deceiving his father (who was old and blind by then) into giving him the spiritual inheritance as well.[14] The fat was in the fire when his trick was discovered. The noise! Esau yelled, 'I'll kill him for this!', Isaac bleated like an ineffectual old billy-goat, and the boys' mother wailed continuously at the top of her voice. Jacob's Guardian managed to get his charge rapidly away to safety by a bit of skilful manipulation,[15] and off he went for an extended visit to his uncle, who lived a very long way away!

Jacob was very miserable indeed as he lay down to sleep on that first night of his long journey. He was terrified that his big thug of a brother would come after him, and he felt ill with homesickness. To be honest, in spite of his acute susceptibility towards us, he really was the wimp his father had always called him! Come to think of it, it often is the Earthlings who are naturally weak and fearful who seem most aware of the heavenly dimension.

As Jacob lay there in the darkness, he felt utterly alone in the world, even though he was completely surrounded by many Guardian Angels.[16] He was the child of promise, you see, however deviously he had come by that privilege, so he had hundreds of them on his case. As he lay wrapped in his cloak, with his head on a hard stone, his worst worry was the feeling that he'd blown it with the Almighty. Because he loved Him so much, all he wanted was to be loved in return. That was the only good quality that Jacob had – everything else about him was bent, mean and acquisitive. But in the Mighty One's eyes that love was all that mattered. He saw the boy lying there in misery, and He couldn't hold himself back – he couldn't even let the boy stew in his own juice for a day or two to teach him a lesson. He drew aside the curtains of Heaven so that Jacob could see what was happening in the real world. As he slept, he saw, in a dream, all the angels that surrounded him, spiralling up and down between Earth and Heaven. He saw them in all their glory, and he was terrified. Earthlings always are! But suddenly he was aware that the Mighty One Himself was standing right beside him.

'I will give you and your descendants the land on which you lie.' He heard the voice distinctly, but he was too afraid to lift his face from the dust which filled his mouth and stung his eyes. He dared not move as the booming voice echoed on, around the craggy rocks, 'Your descendants will be as many as the grains of dust on the earth.' Abraham and Isaac had been looking at the stars when the promise was made to them. Poor Jacob had fallen in the dust and dirt, but the promise was just the same. He was accepted!

'Remember, I will always be with you, I will not leave you until I have done all that I have promised.'

Jacob had several more encounters with angels which I can't stop to tell you about in detail,[17] but I do want to mention one because it will teach you something most important.

When Jacob arrived at his uncle's place he married two of his cousins (unfortunately polygamy was legal then)[18] and settled down to sheep farming. Years went by, and Jacob seemed to forget his angel experience, among the pressures of family life. Even the most susceptible Lighted Ones often become 'Earthbound' when they begin to breed, and their lights dim. Middle age does seem to be the most dangerous stage in any Lighted One's existence. It's not the times of acute hardship or suffering that pull them away from Heaven, but the comforts and successes of life.[19] Well, at first Jacob was *not* comfortable or successful, but he most certainly had lost contact with the Mighty One, as he struggled to feed and clothe his big family on the scanty wages that his mean old uncle paid him.

Then the Mighty One sent a Messenger to do what we call a bit of 'dream-planting'. Remember this – it's important. The minds of Earthlings are most receptive of all to us when they are asleep. The human brain never sleeps, of course, but continues to process information continuously, and so we often find that the best way of communicating is to send messages in the form of a dream. Because Jacob had already encountered the supernatural he knew, as soon as he woke up, that he had been 'visited' again. But a lot of Earthlings simply think they have had a remarkably vivid dream which has given them a new insight, some kind of direction or an inkling of the future. Jacob's dream gave him some remarkable tips on selective breeding, and he was soon an extremely successful farmer – and he also became very rich.[20]

As I say, Jacob had other very dramatic angel experiences and, when he lay dying, his last request to the Mighty One was that the Angel who had guided and protected him from harm throughout his long life would continue to care for his two favourite grandsons.[21] If *only* parents and grandparents would ask the Mighty One more often to surround their offspring with angels.

Sometimes we angels used to shake our heads, totally bewildered, as Jacob's 12 sons grew up. You'd have thought that if the Almighty was going to choose a family to be His own particular possession, He might at least have chosen a nice, quiet, well-behaved one. But no one, not even a deceiver like Lucifer, could describe Jacob's family in those words. They argued, fought, lied and were so jealous and mean that 10 of them finally went so far as to sell the least popular brother to slave-traders for a few coins.[22] They were so mad with that boy that they would have killed him if the traders hadn't come along at the right time. Jacob's sons would do anything for money. But the lad, Joseph, whom they hated so much, was a Lighted One; and all the miseries he went through only caused his inner light to burn more brightly. It's strange, but when things go wrong for those Lighted Ones, their sorrows either act like fuel to their spirit flames or like a damp rug, stifling the fire completely.[23]

Of course, we were all terribly upset as we watched all that Joseph was going through. He was so young, you see, and he felt so totally alone, standing there in that humiliating Egyptian slave-market. He thought no one loved him when he was made to scrub floors and empty chamber-pots, and when he was cuffed, kicked and even beaten.

The real crisis came for him when he was thrown into a dungeon for something he didn't do and was apparently left there to rot, forgotten and abandoned. His wretched loneliness was hard for us to watch but, as I said, he was a Lighted One of the highest rank, so he had a large bodyguard round him all the time. The worse the trauma that a Lighted One is experiencing, the more of us are sent in to help; and our job is to encourage them to *give* their suffering to the Mighty One so that He can use it to their advantage.[24]

Joseph also had more than his fair share of the Others surrounding him as well. They always want to use suffering to turn Lighted Ones against God, and they encourage them to allow bitterness to smother the flame of their spirits. 'If God *really* loved you, He'd look after you a bit better than this,' they whisper to Lighted Ones, just when they're most vulnerable.

In Joseph's dark little prison cell there were hundreds of us, from both sides, fighting over him while he looked so small and helpless. Yet, like all Lighted Ones, *he* was the person who decided which side won the battle!

In Joseph's case he allowed *us* to come out of that battle victorious. He picked himself up off the dungeon floor, kicked off the self-pity which was giving the enemy a toehold, and flatly refused to get upset and angry with the Mighty One.

'I'm going to serve and honour God whether He gets me out of here or not,' he said, and years later we heard him describe that moment as the time when 'iron entered into his soul'.

Naturally, we were all shouting and cheering with joy, and thoroughly enjoyed the sight of Lucifer's Lot limping off to lick their wounds.

Joseph began to reach out to other prisoners, and even to serve them,[25] and eventually it was through one of them that he was set free and given a top-ranking job in the Egyptian government. When he finally met his wicked brothers once again he was able to say, 'You meant all this to harm me, but God meant it to do me good, and it most certainly has.'[26]

Anyway, Jacob, and all 12 of his sons, finally finished up far from the land that God had promised them, and they all died in the place Earthlings call Egypt.[27] But over the next 400 years the family that we were all guarding so carefully developed into the nation it was designed to be, and then the fun really began!

✼

In Egypt they called their kings 'Pharaoh', and a crafty lot most of them were, too! One of them cottoned on to the idea that all the Mighty One's people were so strong and healthy that they would make an excellent workforce. So he sent in Egyptian heavies with big whips and made slaves of all those children of Abraham – the Mighty One's own chosen people! Even you can probably guess who was behind all that! Lucifer has been trying to humiliate and destroy the Jews ever since. We were all thoroughly incensed, but the Mighty One Himself remained silent – biding His time.

So there they all were, slaving away, building artificial mountains called pyramids, fetching and carrying for those Egyptians. And if they so much as muttered a protest, one of those big whips would slash them brutally. It wasn't right! We were getting very restless up here, I can tell you. As a matter of fact, it was the Guardians who really felt the situation most. It was fashionable for every Egyptian home to have a Hebrew slave-child to run errands for them – which, of course, left these little children open to every sort of abuse in the book; and there were masses of temples, all demanding child prostitutes. Then, to cap it all, one Pharaoh launched himself into a genocide programme, which set out to have all male Jewish babies killed at birth – before we angels even had a chance to take charge of them.

'If the Mighty One doesn't do something soon, He won't have a chosen nation left for us to look after,' we thought.

'Why doesn't He get them back to Canaan – the land that he promised would be theirs for ever?'

Warrior Angels were sharpening up their swords and speculating on how many regiments it would take to sort the Egyptians out – permanently. We even had the chariots of fire in formation, ready to transport the Jews over the desert to Canaan. But the Mighty One had already worked out His plan for rescuing the Jews and, as usual, it took us all by surprise.[28]

✱

Gabriel, the Mighty Messenger, was probably more surprised than any of us, and I have to confess that I felt a most unangelic sense of satisfaction when I noticed Him standing in front of the Great Throne looking a bit like a pricked balloon. He does tend to 'know it all', which can be a bit irritating for the rest of us sometimes, and he had looked very pleased with himself when he'd been summoned to the Throne for a briefing session.

'Your Pure Holiness,' he was saying incredulously, 'I am not sure I heard you correctly! Did you *really* say you want me to disguise myself as … *a bonfire?*'

The Mighty One didn't answer, because angels weren't created to ask questions, just to serve. So off Gabriel had to go with a dented ego (well, it would have been dented, if angels *had* egos to dent).

'What's the Mighty One up to now?' we all wondered as we found ourselves spy-holes in the clouds. Gabriel, in spite of his personal feelings, did a good bonfire impersonation,[29] right in the middle of a desert bush. And then the Mighty One Himself spoke through the flames to an ancient, shabby-looking shepherd – a fugitive on the run from Pharaoh, escaping from a murder charge.[30] He'd been wandering aimlessly round in that desert for 40 years, minding someone else's flock of scrawny sheep. He was now so old that he couldn't take a step without his walking stick.

'Go to Egypt and tell Pharaoh to let my people go.' That's what the Mighty One was saying. 'Take them back over this desert and settle them down, snug and cosy, in the land where my friend Abraham lived.'

We wanted to laugh, but we didn't quite dare. At least the old man had some common sense.

'Oh no!' he said. 'I could never do that. I'm nothing but a has-been, a no-good failure. No one would listen to me.'

We heartily agreed, but the Mighty One did *not*.

'Go and get on with it,' He ordered. 'I'll be with you.'

'Why is He putting the poor old man through all this?' we asked Gabriel. 'A job of this size has to be done by angels, or at the very least by a huge army of Earthlings, led by an extremely gifted general. And in desert terrain like this, surely a leader would have to be young, tough and very fit. This poor old man is over 80, stammers badly and lost his self-confidence 40 years ago!'

'Moses can do it,' Gabriel explained. 'He knows the Mighty One so well that they talk face-to-face like two old friends.[31] One old failure of a man who knows how to tap into the resources of Heaven is more powerful than the greatest Earthling army that ever learnt the art of war. You'll see – he'll succeed.'

And, of course, he did. It must have taken a lot of courage to turn up at the door of Pharaoh's palace one day and deliver a ridiculous-sounding message to the most powerful man on earth.[32] Pharaoh was predictably livid, and the Mighty One had to put on a really big show to impress him.

The Family that Shocked Heaven

You never saw such a carry-on – frogs leaping all over the place, gnats biting everyone, swarms of flies, dead cows, boils, hungry locusts, river-water turned to blood, and the worst hailstorm in living memory.[33] The trouble was, the show didn't impress Pharaoh at all – he just wouldn't back down. He wanted to keep those slaves who did all the dirty jobs in the kingdom and never had to be paid any wages. Then, just when we were sure poor old Moses was going to give up for good, the Mighty One sent in his Angels of Judgement to finish Pharaoh off for good and all. During one terrible, dark night, the chief of their division himself, the Angel of Death, moved through the whole country, killing the first-born son in every family.

But this terrible angel never went near the Jewish homes, because they had been told how to protect themselves. Each family had killed a lamb at dusk that evening, and then painted their door-posts with its blood. Whenever that grim angel saw the marks on the door, he passed over the house, and left the children sleeping safely inside. The lamb had died in the place of the eldest son, you see – just as the ram had died to save Isaac.

When the morning came, the outcry in Egypt was terrible. 'Get those Jews out of here!' everyone was screaming at Pharaoh, and he didn't need to be told either, because his own son lay dead.[34]

Notes

1. Gen. 22:1.
2. Isa. 48:17–18.
3. Gen. 4:3–4.
4. Lev. 4:14–15.

5. Gen. 24:1–4.

6. Ps. 91:11, Amplified Version (Zondervan, 1965).

7. Matt. 22:30.

8. Gen. 6:4.

9. Exod. 7:10–12; Rev. 16:14.

10. Gen. 8:1.

11. Gen. 25:20–26.

12. Prov. 12:18.

13. Gen. 21:17.

14. Gen. 27:6–29.

15. Gen. 27:42–46; 28:1–2.

16. Gen. 27:46; 28:1–3.

17. Gen. 32:1–2, 22–32; 35:9–15.

18. Gen. 29:21–28.

19. Deut. 8:11–14.

20. Gen. 31:10–13.

21. Gen. 48:16.

22. Gen. 40:21–22.

23. 2 Cor. 4:16–18.

24. Job 36:15–16.

25. Gen. 40:22–23.

26. Gen. 50:20.

27. Exod. 1:6.

28. 1 Pet. 1:12.

29. Acts 7:30.

30. Exod. 2:14–15.

31. Exod. 33:11.

32. Exod. 7:1–6.

33. Exod. 8 – 10.

34. Exod. 11:5–6.

Chapter 4

The Rumbling Mountain

S o out came the slaves, taking everything they had with them, bundled in sacks on their backs. They took their herds and flocks too, and chickens in baskets, and donkeys weighed down by heavy saddlebags.

It felt like a holiday – at first – a triumphant procession, with the children skipping and dancing and the old folk hopping along on their walking sticks. They were free from slavery at last! We angels led the way, forming a huge column of shining light that Earthlings could actually see, and at night we were allowed to show them the fiery colours of our wings and the burning light of our auras.[1] I was part of that 'pillar of cloud', and it was one of the proudest moments of my life.

We showed the path they were to take each day, and, when we stopped, they camped for the night, and stayed put until we moved on again. It was marvellous fun, being visibly involved for once.

But they hadn't got far down the road before old Pharaoh realized that he had plenty more sons but no more slaves. Who was going to clean the lavatories and build him a new palace? So he came after them, with all his soldiers, chariots and war-horses. The Jews[2] had reached the seaside and were taking a bit of a holiday, paddling in the sea while the children built sand pyramids on the beach. Suddenly they heard the ominous sound of pounding hooves coming nearer by the minute. The sea was in front of them and the hills shut them in on either side.

'We're trapped!' they shouted at Moses. 'We've got nowhere to run!' How could they panic like that, when they could actually *see* a great cloud of angels there to protect them? Extraordinary creatures! Moses calmly told them that they *did* have somewhere to run, and showed them what he meant by falling down flat on his face to pray.

Most Earthlings have the extraordinary idea that the longer they pray, the more effective their prayers will be. Stupid idea! As if the Mighty One needs their words![3] No! Prayers, as soon as they are launched, move out of the realm of time and into eternity where, of course, there are no clocks. A prayer is just as effective against the enemy whether it's made up from thousands of words or just one syllable. In fact the Mighty One hears and reacts to the 'H' of 'Help!' before they even get the whole word out! It's the faith that counts, you see. When a Lighted One looks up into the face of the Mighty One, something indescribable passes between them – too special and private to need words.[4] We angels have nothing in our experience to match it, so it's very hard for me to explain such intimacy. But that's what real prayer is. There are times, of course, when enemy attack is very heavy and the Lighted One will have to go on looking up in faith long enough for us angels to beat the enemy off. Sometimes, during massive celestial battles, that can take weeks! There was one occasion that I remember well, when Michael himself was sent in to engage personally with Lucifer's agent who ruled the Persian Empire.[5] A very brightly burning Lighted One called Daniel was the crucial factor in that skirmish. He had to fast and pray for three weeks before Michael got the victory. If Daniel had stopped praying before that, Michael would have been defeated and the whole of human history would have been totally different. I must keep on stressing to you that we angels can't win any battle without the prayer of an Earthling. Yes, I know how frustrating that sounds, but we have to co-operate with humans in spiritual warfare. We can't manage without them, and, of course, they couldn't possibly manage without us!

✱

But I must go back to poor old Moses, lying face down on the beach while everyone else was yelling abuse at him.

As soon as the old man's prayer arrived, and had been hastily re-launched at the enemy, we angels in the 'pillar' were directed to move to the back of the procession, putting ourselves between the Jews and the Egyptians. The rapidly advancing soldiers couldn't see us, but the Jews were bathed in our soft, celestial light. The four great angels who control the winds[6] had such fun when they were told to blow on the Red Sea and part it in the middle so that the Jews could dash across the mud to safety. But we all enjoyed ourselves when they were ordered to *stop* blowing and we watched the crack regiments of the Egyptian army drown as the water surged back into place. We are so seldom allowed to intervene supernaturally in the affairs of Earthlings, so occasions like that are quite delightful.[7]

Then began the long, slow haul over the scorched wastelands, with us back in the lead. But we often got frustrated by the slowness of those Earthlings. Step after step, plod, plod, plod, plod! Their two-footed pace made us value our wings, I can tell you. Of course, we could have transported those slaves over the desert to their promised land in one second flat, if we'd each picked one up in our arms, but it took them 40 years to walk it.[8] Yet they learned so much in all that time that we had to agree in the end that the Mighty One really did know what He was doing!

But as soon as their food-sacks became empty they complained to poor, harassed old Moses that they were hungry. So, in answer to another of his urgent prayer missiles, we were given a very unusual job to do. Each morning thousands of us were sent out to scatter our own special angel food over the desert sand all round the Jewish campsite.[9] It had never been seen on Earth before, so naturally the Jews were a bit puzzled by it.

'What is it?' they asked each other and, because they couldn't come up with a better name, that's just what they called it – *manna* – which sounds like 'What is it?' in Hebrew. And they loved it – at first.

We distributed the manna before they woke up in the morning, and then they would crawl out of their tents and gather up enough rations for each household for the day. Unfortunately they got extremely sick of it after a while and began yearning for fresh fruit and fried onions. There's a saying down on Earth, 'The way to a man's heart is through his stomach.' Lucifer knows that too, and he uses the human dependence on food to get at them – frequently. His Lot can dream-plant too, as well as thought-plant, and they bombarded those Jews with visions of delicious food until they were positively dribbling.

'It was great back in Egypt,' they would mutter. 'All those juicy melons, and just remember all that gorgeous wine!' But no one mentioned the whips and hard labour.

If there's one thing the Mighty One really hates, it's grumbling discontent. I suppose it's because complaining is such a joy-robber, and He loves to see the people He loves bubbling with happiness. And they *can be*, in almost any situation, provided they are determined *not to grouse*.[10] When you're sent to Earth you'll find that the sound of their endless murmuring is very ugly to angel ears, like a constant discordant drone. They think they are being very daring and honest, but really it's anger against the Almighty and it hurts Him profoundly.[11] They feel so sorry for themselves that they lose all compassion for others, and don't see the effect that their complaining actually has on everybody else's joy levels. I'm glad angels weren't created to grumble, just to serve.

About three months after they left Egypt something very important happened. The ex-slaves arrived at the mountain they call Sinai, where Gabriel had disguised himself as a burning bush. It's not much of a mountain by Heaven's standards – just bare, rugged rocks, riddled with caves and wrapped round by gloomy clouds – but the Mighty One beckoned Moses to come up and meet Him at the top.

'Go and tell the people to wash themselves and change their clothes,' He told Moses, 'because in three days' time I'm coming down from Heaven in all my glory to talk to them on this mountain.' He wanted to give them those ten great Rules of Happiness which I told you about earlier.[12]

'We don't want to hear God speak!' bleated the terrified Jews. 'We'd *much* rather not meet Him in person.' That's typical of Earthlings, by the way. The one thing the Mighty One wants is an intimate relationship with each one of them, but most of them back off – fast – when they think He's getting too close.

Anyway, they all had to line up round the foot of the mountain, teeth chattering, knees knocking. And when they were all assembled – at least three million of them – we put on our finest celestial show. The Cherubim shook the mountain until its rocks rattled, while the Seraphim played their instruments loudly enough to deafen half the world. We working-class angels organized the thunder and lightning, the four Wind Angels blew a gale,[13] and the Angel of Fire set the whole mountain ablaze.[14] Smoke belched out between the rocks, while 10,000 of us swirled and danced in the air round the summit. Then the trumpets began – they can't half make a noise, that Seraphim brass band!

Gigantic blasts heralded the arrival of the Mighty One Himself, dressed in a thick, black cloud. Awesome, that's what we were! Those poor Jews! Most of them fell senseless to the ground in sheer terror, while others shook so much that they couldn't stand up and collapsed on top of the others. Even Moses was scared. No other Earthling in the history of the world has ever seen anything like our performance that day. It was a big occasion for the entire planet, which had to be suitably marked. The great Creator came to Earth to make an everlasting pact with His people. If they obeyed His Ten Rules of Happiness He would take care of them for ever. If not...

As we swirled round Sinai we angels told each other, 'After this, Earthlings will *never* dare to disobey or ignore the

Mighty One again, not now that they've seen just how powerful He really is!'

Earthlings have remarkably short memories for such intelligent beings! If only they'd kept those simple Rules of Happiness there would have been no swords down there on Earth, and no guns or bombs either. Soldiers and prisons would have been unnecessary, and so would most hospitals and doctors. There wouldn't have been any famines because nations would have shared their resources. Guardian Angels would have had an easy time, because children would never have been abused, and women would never have been raped, battered or used as prostitutes. There would have been no loneliness or rejection, no divorce or desertion, no forced labour or refugee camps, no greedy rich people, no bullies or tyrants, not much illness and no stress-related diseases. Most of the suffering which Earthlings endure is caused because someone else doesn't love them as much as they love themselves. Yes, if only ... but, of course, Lucifer still rules the Earth.

It wasn't long before they were grumbling again, and this time the Mighty One had to unleash the Angel of Death to teach them a lesson.[15] That's *not* a nice story, so all I'll say is that it took them 40 years to learn to trust the Mighty One enough to be allowed into the land they'd been promised.

✱

As we led them nearer to Canaan something very funny happened. We angels love to tell the story – when we're off duty, of course. The land which the Mighty One had given to Abraham had long been overrun by various tribes, who were always fighting each other and who had some disgusting

An Angel Called Mervin

habits. They openly worshipped Lucifer under the name of Baal, killed their children as ritual sacrifices to him, and mated with animals because they thought producing monsters was fun! Yes, it was a dirty place and many of their cities were little better than Sodom. The Angels of Judgement were impatient to go down and clean the whole place up, but the Mighty One said He intended to use the Jews to do the job for Him this time.

Of course, those Canaanite tribes were not very pleased when the rumours began to reach them that millions of people were tramping across the desert in their direction, with every intention of living in their homes and harvesting their fields. Very cross indeed, they were, but one of their kings had a bright idea. There was a man in those parts called Balaam[16] whose psychic powers gave him a huge reputation. He was a Lighted One, even though he was not a Jew, and he was also extremely susceptible to the supernatural. The Caananite king decided to hire him to curse the Jews – offering him a huge financial reward. At least Earthlings in those days had enough sense to realize the power a curse can have – or a blessing, for that matter. Balaam was flattered, and he asked the Mighty One, 'Can I do this?'

'Definitely *not!*' was His prompt answer. 'Stay right where you are and ignore the king.'

But the king kept on at Balaam, offering him such vast sums of money that, in the end, the stupid man saddled up his faithful old donkey and set off with the king's emissaries. He was hoping that the Mighty One would change his mind before he reached the Jewish camp.

Of course, there was no way the Mighty One was going to let anyone curse His own chosen people, so a very big Warrior Angel was sent to bar the donkey's path – with his drawn sword flashing in the sunshine. The donkey saw him at once and stopped dead, his eyeballs rolling with fear. The poor creature made a quick dash through a gate into a nearby field – anything to get away from that angel. I've already told you that animals can see us far more easily than Earthlings. A horse, dog or cat will look up at a Messenger or a Guardian and show fear or curiosity, and as we move about they'll follow us with their eyes. The Earthling who owns them may not see us, but the animal's reaction tells them that something supernatural is happening.

Many Earthlings are just as stupid as Balaam. He didn't stop to ask himself why his donkey was behaving like that. He lost his cool completely, jumped off, beat the poor animal and then clambered back into the saddle.

Cautiously the donkey moved on again, picking its way along the stony little path between the vineyards. Balaam was still feeling cross, and we weren't surprised, because we could see the way his Angel of Conscience was pricking him in the heart. He *wanted* all the money that the king was offering, but he knew he was going against the Mighty One's wishes.

Just round the next corner the path narrowed between two stone walls and there, almost filling the gap, stood the angel once again. The donkey tried to make a dash between the angel and the stone wall, but he was an old donkey and blind in one eye, so he badly misjudged the gap. Balaam's foot was rammed against the dry-stone wall. Bellowing with rage and pain, he extricated himself and then, hopping and hobbling all over the path, he cursed his donkey until it brayed loudly in protest.

'If I had a sword I'd kill you!' fumed Balaam. 'Can't you see I'm in a hurry to meet the king?'

Then he beat his donkey all over again, and finally eased his bleeding leg back over the saddle, and kicked the donkey into action.

'This time you're going to behave,' he warned menacingly.

But round the next corner there was the Warrior once again, standing in such a narrow place on the path that even the half-blind donkey could see there was no room to get by – and no space to turn round and run for it either! So the poor old animal gave up completely and lay down on the path – squashing Balaam's good foot as he did so. That did it! Balaam attacked his donkey so viciously that we all thought he'd kill it this time.

We hate to see animals hurt and needlessly ill treated, and we are often sent to comfort them. The Mighty One has a corner of his heart for everything he created, and I've seen him weep over the unnecessary death of a field-mouse, a wood-vole or a dusty little town sparrow.[17] He seemed to have had quite enough of Balaam and his cruelty by that time, so He gave the donkey the power to speak – an unheard-of thing in Earth's history.

'Master, can't you see that there's a great big angel in the way?' said the donkey.

Balaam was in such a state by that time that he was not even surprised to hear his own donkey talking. Stress has the strangest effect on these Earthlings.

'I'm the same old donkey you've ridden since you were a little boy,' continued the animal, 'so why do you think I'm behaving out of character like this all of a sudden?'

'I haven't the slightest idea!' growled Balaam, and then he froze. He looked down at his donkey, all matted with blood, sweat and dust, gazing at him in bewilderment. Then the Mighty One let him see the Warrior Angel too, standing over him with a deep frown of disapproval on his face. The sharp end of his great sword was pointing right at Balaam, almost touching his neck.

'Why have you beaten your poor donkey like this?' he demanded. 'If he had not prevented you from riding into me I would have run my sword right through you. But be sure I would have spared your donkey, because he has much more sense than you have!' Balaam threw himself face down in front of the angel.

'I'm sorry,' he moaned. 'I give up. I know the Almighty has sent you. I won't curse these people, for He's obviously on their side. I'll go straight home, I promise.'

'No you won't,' replied the Angel coolly. 'You'll go on and meet the king, but you'll only say what the Mighty One tells you to say.'

A few days later, a huge gathering of the tribes and clans took place on a high vantage spot overlooking the flat lands where the Jews had made camp. They were there for the cursing ceremony, and rows of witches and wizards, and other servants of Lucifer, were chanting and prancing about, to build the atmosphere of tension. Chieftains and clan leaders waited in rows to see the great man himself at work. Balaam, of course, was centre stage, but was beginning to wish that he was anywhere else in the whole world. Right to the last moment he hoped that the Mighty One would change His mind and let him do a nice, juicy curse. He ought to have realized that no Earthling who has the protection of the Mighty One can be harmed by any curse from the enemy.[18]

He stood there, hoping to spout the speech that would make him rich for the rest of his life, but he suddenly remembered that huge angel who had blocked his path. He rolled his eyes to look at the king standing next to him, and

An Angel Called Mervin

he made a big discovery. The sight of a Warrior Angel was far more terrifying than the rage of any earthly king! So he opened his mouth, and the Mighty One filled it with the most extravagant blessings that Balaam had ever uttered. Naturally, the king was livid, and Balaam never got his rich reward. The donkey brayed happily, and we angels have been chuckling ever since.

✤

As I said, it took us 40 years to get the Jews over the desert to their 'Land of Promise'. But, to be honest, we angels were amazed as we watched the Mighty One changing that rabble of cringing slaves into an efficient force of highly trained, well-organized fighting men. Moses was never the great charismatic leader we would have chosen for the job, but he could distinguish the voice of the Mighty One better than most Earthlings who ever lived.[19] So all he had to do was follow orders; it really was the Mighty One Himself who did it all, and no one else can take any credit.

It did seem sad that Moses blew his chance to lead the people right into the land,[20] but his impatience caused his love for the people to fail on one significant occasion. The Mighty One can't tolerate lack of love; so the old man's assistant Joshua was the Mighty One's choice for the final push into Canaan. Moses was heartbroken, naturally. He had so looked forward to seeing the land full of rich pasture and exotic flowers and fruit. The thought had kept him going all the way through that dismal desert. As usual, the Mighty One relented and told him to climb to the peak of Mount Nebo.[21]

'You'll have a perfect view of Canaan from up there,' He promised. 'And then I'll send my angels to fetch you home.'[22]

We watched the old man carefully picking his way up the steep mountainside. He'd reached the time of life when most Earthlings sit in rocking-chairs reminiscing, but Moses was used to mountains. When he reached the summit he shaded his eyes with a shaky, gnarled old hand and took an angel-eye view of Canaan laid out at his feet: green valleys, rushing rivers and gentle hills covered with silvery olive groves. You just keep on hoping you'll be sent on many an assignment to Israel. Moses wept with joy when he saw it all at last.

And then the Archangel Michael and a platoon of his finest Warriors were sent to collect him and bring him home. You'll soon discover that the greatest excitement we angels ever have comes when a Lighted One gets the royal summons.[23] Unlit Earthlings call it death, and dread it as the end of everything. The Lighted Ones know different – or they *should*!

When their time on Earth comes to an end, a special escort is despatched at once to carry the soul and spirit up here carefully in their arms, or even on their wings.[24] (Sometimes this angelic escort is mistaken for a coach and horses made of fire.)[25] As they approach, the gates are flung wide and their new body is hurried out to them. Earthlings don't bring their old body with them because it's often so worn out, disease-ridden or damaged that they wouldn't want it anyway. And, of course, Earthling bodies, even when they are in perfect shape, are ridiculously limited, so they definitely need a new one. They look exactly like the old ones did, but they can do so much more.[26] We always laugh with joy at their pleasure when they discover that they can bounce high in the air and turn somersaults, and they can fly and float about on the clouds. Some of them have been trapped for years in bodies that hurt or wouldn't move properly, so the sheer ecstasy of movement completely intoxicates them at first.

As they move through the gates they are met by a royal welcoming party[27] – massed bands play; choirs sing anthems of triumph; bells ring out all over Heaven; trumpeters blare huge fanfares; troups of dancers tumble and twirl exuberantly; and, of course, there are cheering crowds of witnesses. (They are Lighted Ones who have already arrived and have been cheering them on during their earthly life.)[28] Their applause and roars of welcome can be almost deafening.[29]

Sometimes the expression on the faces of these newly arrived Lighted Ones can be hilarious. Often they were totally ignored on Earth – written off as old, disabled, poor or even fools.[30] Yet they may have ignited thousands of spirits by their prayer missiles; brought down governments; changed the course of history; and all the time everyone thought they were doing nothing but lying forgotten in a bed, sitting despised in a wheelchair or chained to a dungeon wall. When such people are greeted with a grade-one heavenly welcome, you can't blame them for looking astonished.

Generally, though, Lighted Ones of such high rank don't even look at the welcome committee. They run straight past all the angels and make a dash for the Mighty One's throne – like eager children home from boarding school for the holidays. All through their lives they've been yearning to see His face, and they just can't wait.[31] They never reach the throne, of course – He couldn't possibly wait that long! He rushes down to meet them halfway, arms held out in ecstatic welcome.

Be prepared – the first few times you see it happen, it will hurt, because, you see, we angels can never share that relationship with the Mighty One. You'll feel a strange pang of longing, because He never wraps us angels in His arms like that.[32] We are servants, created to serve and say 'Holy, Holy, Holy' with bowed heads, but they can smile into His face.

The relationship He has with some of those Earthlings is so close that it can't possibly be understood in Heaven or on Earth. The Mighty One sometimes tries to explain it to them by saying He wants them to look on Him as a much-loved parent,[33] or even a doting husband, but even these models are totally inadequate to explain the intimacy He offers them.

He even gives each of them a private nickname! He writes it on a little white stone and slips it into their hands when they arrive up here.[34] They keep that stone so carefully and gloat over it secretly. It gives them such joy, you see, because it shows them that they are unique, not just one of a great big crowd, easily lost and forgotten. No, the Mighty One knows their own secret pet name, and when He whispers it they come to enjoy His undivided attention. We angels can never approach Him like that. It's no good feeling bad about that, but it *does* upset us when these Earthlings simply do not understand how favoured they are.

There's probably something else which will puzzle you when you first go to Earth, and that's the way that Lighted Ones pray urgently when one of their friends is so ill that they seem to be dying. They get together in their church prayer meetings and pray until they sweat, and sometimes it sounds to us as if they thought death was the *worst* thing that could happen. If they could once see a heavenly welcoming party in progress, they would realize that dying is the best moment in any Lighted Earthling's life![35]

Of course, the arrival of some Lighted Ones at the gates can be quite funny. Occasionally one turns up expecting a massive welcome because he or she has been considered very great down below – people such as important Church leaders, well-known philanthropists, writers of famous books, founders of respected organizations. But all their achievements don't count for much up here if they didn't have love in their hearts for the Mighty One.[36] Some are so busy *serving* Him, you see, that they get their priorities all wrong.[37] By the end of their lives on Earth they have become so famous and revered that the flame of love for the Mighty One Himself has dwindled almost to nothing, stifled by pride and self-respect. They don't realize that it's not achievements He rewards but faithfulness.

So instead of the ecstatic ceremonies of welcome that they were used to on Earth, they walk in here virtually unnoticed. The Mighty One is always very nice to them – He has no favourites. But so often it isn't *Him* they're anxious to see when they get up here – they're eager to be fitted for their crown, or they demand to see the grand mansion that they expect to be given.

But we need to go back to Moses, because Lucifer fought to get him, right to the last. How the Others hated that gentle old man! You'll hardly believe this, but just as Michael himself was gathering Moses up in his arms to bring him home, who should turn up but Lucifer, in person.[38] He doesn't often bother to appear on Earth, but this time, there he was, yelling abuse, threats and insults.

'You give him to me, Michael!' he demanded. Now here's another lesson you need to learn. We angels never answer Lucifer back. We always treat him with politeness because he is still the highest-ranking angel in the universe – and anyway, angels weren't created to argue, just to serve. We know that one day the Mighty One will deal with him,[39] and that day is worth waiting for! So never be tempted to get into a shouting match with one of the Others. They can out-argue anyone, and they are all masters in the art of lying.[40]

So Michael simply would not listen to Lucifer's threats. He lifted Moses into his great, powerful arms, and he and his troop of angels rocketed back to Heaven in grand style.

Notes

1. Exod. 13:21–22.
2. The Bible does not call Abraham's descendants Jews at this stage, but for the sake of simplicity I have called Israelis by that name throughout this book.
3. Matt. 6:7–8.
4. S. of S. 2:14; Job 22:26–27.
5. Dan. 10:13.
6. Rev. 7:1.
7. Exod. 14:24–28.
8. Josh. 5:6.
9. Ps. 78:25.
10. Phil. 4:12.
11. Ps. 78:40–41.
12. Exod. 20:1–17.
13. Rev. 7:1.
14. Rev. 8:7.
15. 1 Cor. 10:10.
16. Num. 22 – 24.
17. Matt. 10:29.
18. Isa. 54:17.
19. Heb. 3:5.
20. Num. 20:1–12.
21. Deut. 32:48–52; 34:1–5.
22. Jude 9.
23. Ps. 116:15.
24. Luke 16:22.

25. 2 Kings 2:11.
26. Phil. 3:20–21.
27. Rev. 14:13.
28. Heb. 12:1.
29. Isa. 36:10.
30. Matt. 19:28–30.
31. Ps. 17:15.
32. Isa. 43:4.
33. Isa. 49:15–16; 54:5.
34. Rev. 2:17.
35. Phil. 1:21–23.
36. 1 Cor. 13:1–3.
37. Matt. 6:1–4.
38. Jude 9.
39. Rom. 16:20.
40. John 8:44.

Chapter 5

War and Peace

Moses' promotion to Heaven left his assistant Joshua facing a tricky military situation.[1] He had to drive hordes
of fierce tribesmen and guerrilla fighters out of their
own familiar terrain, using troops who had never seen real
action in their lives. And some of the enemy soldiers were as
tall as giants![2] The Mighty One told Joshua to wipe them out
completely, leaving no pockets of resistance to cause trouble
later.[3] The poor man's heart must have sunk as he faced the
prospect of his first objective – taking the fortified city of
Jericho. Not only was it surrounded by high walls, but it was
garrisoned by highly trained fighting men, armed to the
teeth. The city gates were tightly barred and they had enough
provisions to withstand a siege of months. Joshua had no
supplies at all. We weren't even delivering the manna any
more by then.[4] He couldn't afford to hang about, nor could he
think of a single way to breach those thick, stone walls.

One evening he left the Jewish camp and went out at twilight for a walk by himself.[5] He had thought through, and rejected, so many different strategic plans, each one more impossible than the last, and his tired brain couldn't come up with any more. He walked in the direction of Jericho, feeling that it might help to take a closer look at his objective. Suddenly he froze, the hair on the back of his neck rising as the soldier in him reached for his weapon. A giant figure was standing in his path, motionless in the dusk, but he saw the glint of metal. He was obviously a soldier and he was holding a sword. For a full minute Joshua stood there weighing him up, trying to decide if he should attack or run for his life. He was huge, almost twice as tall as Joshua, and even in the fading light he could see the bulging muscles in his powerful shoulders. His legs were planted well apart, and the sword was unsheathed and held in front of him. Joshua could see that he would be no match for this man of war, but the idea of running like a coward revolted him. So, gripping his own sword tightly, he stepped forward and croaked, 'Who goes there – friend or foe?'

'Neither!' rang out the reply. 'I am here as the commander of the Lord's army!' Of course, it was none other than the Archangel Michael himself, chief of all the Warrior Angels. He had also been given the special job of Guardian to the new nation of Israel. Joshua fell face down on the ground in front of him.

'Sir,' he gasped, 'I'm your servant. What do you want me to do?'

'Take your sandals off,' replied Michael. 'This place is holy.'

Now, at that moment, Joshua was in great danger of worshipping Michael. I know I've told you this already, but it's vital that you remember *not to let Earthlings worship you*. Only the Mighty One Himself is worthy of that, so don't let the awe of Earthlings go to your heads. Remember Lucifer? His pride came before his fall!

You'll find Earthlings praying to us angels too. They prefer Michael because of his power, but any of us will do when they're in a tight corner.[6] Those prayers get nowhere at all. They rise into the atmosphere and are picked off by the first sniper who spots them, because they are phoney prayers, with a faulty address.

Anyway, back to Joshua. As he knelt barefoot in the dust, Michael gave him a detailed battle-plan for taking Jericho and, before the interview was over, managed to convince him that during the many other battles that lay ahead, he, Michael, and his hosts would be there fighting beside the Jewish armies.[7]

Joshua finally walked home as dawn broke, whistling confidently. After all, with the assistance of such a mighty army, how could he possibly fail? And he didn't!

Mind you, his soldiers must have been a well-disciplined bunch, or there would have been a mutiny during the following week as Joshua put Michael's instructions into practice. Those poor Jews must have felt ridiculous marching round and round the walls of Jericho in complete silence – except for endless blasts on those wretched trumpets they had made out of animal horns. (The noise would set the teeth of a Seraph on edge – if the Seraphim *had* any teeth.) Every day it was the same – 'left-right, left-right, tramp-tramp, toot-toot' – then back home to bed – and all done in an eerie silence that we could see was unnerving the garrison inside the walls and causing their filthy armpits to prickle with fear.

Joshua's soldiers had no way of seeing the effect that their tactics were having, and some of his sergeants must have wondered if he'd mislaid his marbles while he was out on that midnight hike. Those ghastly rams' horns were enough to get anyone down, and morale hit rock bottom by the end of the week. Then, on the seventh day, Joshua briefed his troops carefully.

'Its D-Day today, lads,' he said (or something like that, anyway). 'When I give the signal, shout your heads off, and then get ready to beat the daylights out of Jericho.'

Mystified, but obedient, they set off for the usual route march and trumpeting session. The columns of men stretched right round the city, circling it completely, and when Joshua dropped his arm the shouting swept through the ranks, enclosing the city in ear-shattering, blood-curdling noise. Behind the Jewish troops was an outer ring of Warrior Angels, unseen by the Earthlings. When the shouting began, they stepped forward over the Earthlings' heads and each one pushed a section of the walls inwards.

The great boulders fell effortlessly under their mighty strength, as if they were made of nothing more solid than polystyrene (which, of course, hadn't even been invented at that stage of Earth's history). With a great rumbling roar and clouds of dust, the walls collapsed. Joshua's soldiers swarmed over them and took the city without resistance. The Warrior Angels stood looking on, smiling affectionately – like parents watching a school football match.

After that Joshua didn't need too much supernatural help. He and his men did a splendid job for many years. In the end, though, success did make them a bit soft, and they decided not to bother with some enemy villages in the back-woods, or the settlements right up in the hills.[8]

'We can't go traipsing round the back of beyond,' they

said. 'We want to start work on our new farms. Let's leave them to get on with it – they can't do much harm, surely.'

But they forgot that the Mighty One had told them to cleanse the *whole* land of everyone who worshipped his enemy Lucifer. If His people were to be a perfect example of the 'good life' to the rest of the world, they must be free of any danger of contamination. Earthlings always underestimate the danger of Lucifer's followers, and the Jews hung up their swords a little bit too soon.

✻

When Joshua was an old man he did see another angel, but it wasn't a very happy occasion. This time the angel was *not* disguised as a man, and it wasn't Michael either – it was the chief of the Messenger Angels, Gabriel.[9] He stepped down to Earth at a place called Gilgal, and immediately attracted a vast crowd of startled spectators. He towered high above their heads in the full dress-uniform of Heaven – dazzling white clothes and plumage of indescribable colours. He stood at the crossroads, waiting, motionless, as more and more people gathered round gaping at him in silent wonder. Then slowly and majestically he began to move down the road, keeping a couple of metres off the ground. The news of his presence spread like wildfire, and people threw down their hoes and sickles, left the herds half milked and the olives ungathered, and they ran from all directions to join the silent procession. By the time they reached a vast natural amphitheatre at a placed called Bokim, everyone who was anyone in the land had arrived, and finally the ancient figure of Joshua was carried up on a litter. It was a very far cry from that night years before when he'd met Michael.

'This is the message from the Lord High God,' began Gabriel in a voice that carried for miles and echoed round all the hilltops in the area. He has a great sense of occasion, but some of us feel that he lacks the common touch.

'I took you out of Egypt and brought you to the land that I promised to your ancestors. I said I would never break my side of the bargain that I made with Abraham, and again with you at Mount Sinai, but you must be careful to keep your side if you want My help and protection. I told you to destroy all the people of the land, but you have not done so. Beware! They will be deadly enemies, and you will be trapped by the worship of their gods.'

Gabriel brought his impressive speech to a dramatic end by melting away before their eyes – leaving his cowering audience in tears. How they regretted their disobedience! For years after that they all worked hard to keep the Mighty One's Rules, and they managed very well while there were still people old enough to remember that incredible journey from Egypt.

✱

But time went by. The Jews grew rich and successful. A new generation grew up who'd never seen supernatural things happening.[10] They had always known peace and prosperity, and during such times the spirits of men seem so comfortable that they sleep and their lights grow dim. It's when they lose all their little props and comforts that they long for Heaven and their lights burn bright. When they can actually see what their losses are doing for their lights, and start thanking the Mighty One for allowing those losses – well, then their radiance becomes positively dazzling.[11]

Of course, this presents the Mighty One with a real dilemma. Because He loves his Lighted Ones so much, He longs to lavish on them every kind of blessing imaginable – health, wealth, peace and freedom – yet the more He gives them, the more likely they are to turn from Him and concentrate on enjoying His blessings.[12] We angels feel so sad for Him over this.

It was at this time of national complacency and cosiness that Lucifer saw his chance. He had his followers among those little groups of people whom the early Jewish settlers had left holed up in odd corners of Canaan, and he began to use them to infiltrate the Jewish communities.[13] Many even married Jewish girls. Lucifer's clever! He knows that an enemy who looks like a friend is far more dangerous than the ferocious-looking kind that you can spot a mile off. Many of his followers posed as 'Modern Thinkers' and 'Free Minds':

'Perhaps all those old stories our grannies used to tell were a bit exaggerated,' they told groups of students and would-be intellectuals. 'Bread from Heaven? Clouds made of angels? Talking donkeys? Who's ever *seen* an angel, anyway? Moses and Joshua were just great natural leaders who made up stories about the supernatural in order to increase their own political power, in the days when people were ignorant enough to be superstitious. All that stuff about Yahweh – it's old hat now! Who wants to worship in that shabby old tent that Moses designed, or to be bossed around by moth-eaten old priests? Most of them are hypocrites anyway. Get back to nature – worship under the trees and out on the hillsides.[14] Be free! Rediscover primitive life-forces. Search for good old Mother Earth. Let's get into the New Age and leave all those restrictive "thou-shalt-nots" behind us.'

Lucifer even got them quoting his favourite clichés: 'You wanna be free, man! Let it all hang out! Do your own thing and be good to yourself.'[15] Like I've said before, Earthlings fall for that unoriginal old stuff every time. Soon the younger generation were worshipping Baal and Ashtoreth, not realizing that they were only fancy names for Lucifer himself.[16] The Ten Rules of Happiness were considered so old fashioned that they were not even mentioned.

The inevitable result was misery. It always is when people stop loving the Mighty One and putting Him first. Soon the country was ruled by greedy, power-hungry bullies.[17]

The odd thing is that when the lives of Earthlings go wrong they usually turn round and blame the Mighty One, as if it was all His fault.[18]

'If He's a God of love,' they shout, 'why does He allow all this suffering?' They never seem to blame the right person, and fail to realize that Lucifer's gang are having a celebration party at their expense.

Soon it was a good way of 'keeping up with the Joneses' for a family to build their own shrine to Baal, and his priests encouraged them to take their little girls to his temples for dancing lessons. To be a temple dancer was a prestigious career for girls, as well as boys, but it really meant high-class prostitution. Fortune-telling, calling up demons masquerading as spirits of the dead, and occult practices of all kinds became popular 'family fun', and ritual human sacrifices were back once again, and the craze was spreading like wildfire.[19]

What was the point of all the Mighty One's efforts, we thought, as we sadly shook our heads. He should have left them to rot in Egypt. But He didn't give up on them. He couldn't, could He? He's Love.

The sad thing is that when Earthlings break one of His Rules, it's always a failure of love – either love for Him or for another Earthling[20] – and failing to love bars them from coming up here to Heaven when their earthly life is over. You may well be wondering how any of them *ever* managed to get up here at all! But remember, if they said they were sorry, and then put their guilt onto a lamb who was killed in their place,[21] they could be pronounced innocent, whatever evil they had done.

Don't go getting the wrong idea. In spite of the spread of Lucifer's lies, there are always those who decide to love the Mighty One and commit themselves to obeying His Rules of love for other people. Whenever an Earthling first makes that decision, and their spirit 'lights up', it fills Him with such joy that we angels have a celebration.[22] We dance all over Heaven with sheer delight at His pleasure. Fanfares blast, anthems roar like waves crashing on a million beaches, and clouds of joy, like soap bubbles, float all over Heaven. Those parties are the best fun we ever have, and we all attend the ceremonial Name Writing. I haven't told you about that yet, have I? In a vast hall near the Majestic Throne Room is the largest book in the universe.[23]

It contains all the names of those who have given the love of their hearts to the Mighty One. How He prizes that book! Sometimes, when He feels sad or discouraged, He'll go in there all alone and read those names out loud to Himself, pausing over each one, and smiling tenderly as He thinks about the person concerned.

But back to work! Whenever the majority of His people turned away from Him, the Mighty One officially withdrew His support and called off the Warrior Angels who were posted all round the national boundaries. Once they were gone, there was nothing to stop the neighbouring nations from attacking the Jews. So in they swarmed, unhindered, and seized power – stealing everything in sight. Soon the Jews were in great distress as their homes were burnt down and their land was taken over by strangers.

Then the people would bleat to the Mighty One for help, and He would empower one of his Lighted Ones to rescue them.[24] These men would be given Warrior Angels to assist them, as well as natural gifts of leadership, and soon the enemies would be driven out and peace would be re-established. The people would be so grateful that a time of spiritual renewal always followed, and everyone would behave nicely – for a while. But it never lasted long. When they were fat and prosperous again, their young would soon start listening to the same old lies and clichés, until a fresh disaster would bring them back to their senses. And so the dismal cycle continued throughout the next thousand years. What fools those Jews were! They could have ruled the world, if only …

✱

Perhaps even the Mighty One Himself might have abandoned His whole plan, but for the few who went on loving Him. To Him, everything seems worth it when He hears their voices chattering away to Him from Earth. If ever you're on duty near enough to the Mighty One to hear one of these conversations, take a peep through your wing feathers and just see how His face lights up with love and joy. If only Lighted Ones knew just how much pleasure it gives Him when they actually spend time with Him, sharing their funny little lives with Him. If they could see His face, as we can, they would certainly spend as much time with Him as possible.

Now, I hope I haven't confused you here. I'm not talking about those missile prayers of intercession,[25] but the kind of thing that Lighted Ones call 'praise' – telling Him how much they love and appreciate Him – thanking Him for all that He's done.[26] Praise like that wafts up towards Heaven like exquisitely fragrant drops of perfume,[27] which are gathered carefully by junior Seraphim who distil the precious liquid into large bowls. Each evening they present these bowls to the Mighty One, and *how* He enjoys it. In fact, it gives Him quite acute pleasure. Each separate droplet of praise is important to Him, but some have a higher quality of perfume than others. Praise that rises from huge, excited congregations of massed Lighted Ones is generally of quite low quality. You see, humans find praising easy when they're all hyped up emotionally by a huge crowd. But the kind of praise which comes from hospital beds, prison cells[28] and lonely, forgotten people who have nothing going for them – yet they *still praise* through clenched teeth and out of a broken heart – that's high-quality praise! It has such a remarkably sweet scent that you'll hear Him murmur, 'She *really* said that about me?' or 'Fancy him being able to say that when ...' People who give Him pleasure like that are quite the most important people on Earth, but, of course, no one down there ever realizes that! You'll often see other little lights appearing in clusters all round these Bright Lights wherever they move on the Earth's surface, simply because they influence others. Their love for the Mighty One ignites humans' spirits like nothing else.[29]

Lucifer's hate for these VIPs is passionate. You'll see his agents surrounding them constantly, always watching for the slightest chance to snuff out their light, or at least cause temporary dimming.[30] But you'll also see that Lighted Ones who are gifted in the art of prayer have a much larger body-guard than, say, preachers, pastors or organizers of church activities. Pray-ers always out-rank anyone else on Earth.

By the way, Lighted Ones have been given the authority to speak to, and even give orders to, demons (provided that they only ever do so in the Mighty One's name).[31] They have no authority to order us to do anything, but they can command the Others to leave their home inside a human, or give up their control over situations. They can gag demons too, and bind them in chains – just by a word which the nasty creatures have to obey,[32] and they can even send them off to temporary imprisonment in the Abyss, which is a very nasty jail for fallen angels.[33] It seems strange to us that such limited, foolish little creatures as humans should have been given such power but, fortunately for Lucifer, most of them never think of using it.

※

One day Michael himself was called to the Presence and told to prepare for a trip to Earth. It had been centuries since any of us had been allowed to appear down there or speak audibly to a human, because belief in the supernatural had been dim for so long. The arrogant antics of the Jews had caused the Mighty One to call the Big Guys off protection duty, and the Land had been invaded by yet another horde of raiders called Midianites.[34] These thugs rode fast camels and what they couldn't kill, eat or rape, they burnt to ashes. But there was at least one very Bright Light in Israel at that time. As usual, no one on Earth had a clue how important he was in the heavenly economy, particularly himself! He was the youngest son of an insignificant farmer, from a small village miles from anywhere. But that young man was the kind of pray-er I've just been telling you about. His name was Gideon.

'I want you to go to him,' the Mighty One told Michael. 'I have chosen him to set my people free.'

This time the Great Angel did not look like a magnified edition of an Earthling soldier. He wore the disguise of an itinerant preacher – and a very shabby one at that. He positioned himself under an oak tree, above the disused winepress where Gideon was grinding wheat.

This young Earthling had a confidence problem – in fact he didn't have any confidence at all! What he *did* have was a very nervous temperament and a father who'd called him a runt from birth. In fact, to Michael, he looked more like a tremulous little field-mouse than a man, kneeling there in the shadows, doing a job usually left to women. The angel's great booming voice, in the silence of the hot afternoon, sent the poor young man sprawling backwards in sheer terror.

'Hail, strong, brave soldier!' said Michael. I must confess, to those of us watching, that greeting did not seem entirely appropriate for a gibbering wreck in the middle of a major panic attack!

'Who? Me?' squeaked the poor young man. If I'd been Michael I'd have used a gentle whisper, but then I'm not an Archangel, am I? Of course, Gideon had no idea he was being addressed by one, because on top of his dirty old clothes Michael was even sporting a long, matted beard and flowing white hair.

'Go, for the Lord is with you,' boomed Michael. 'Rid the land of all these Midianite intruders.'

'What, me?' gasped poor Gideon again. 'What could a nobody like me do against all those war-camels? Why, there are so many of them, they're like a plague of locusts swarming everywhere.'

'Go in the strength that you have,' was the angel's calm reply.

'That's just the point. I don't *have* any strength,' protested poor little Gideon. Typical! Like I said, if Lighted Ones knew that all the strength of Heaven is theirs for the asking, they'd attempt the impossible every day before lunch!

Suddenly Gideon's protests died away as he took a closer look at the figure under the oak tree. He was beginning to shimmer with an unearthly light and his appearance was subtly changing.

'Lord,' Gideon whispered respectfully, 'how can I save Israel?'

Michael looked up to the Mighty One and was told exactly how to reply.

'You can do it, because I will be with you,' was the message. Gideon swallowed hard. His teachers at school had told him that angels did not exist, but ... suppose they were wrong. Could this even be God Himself?

'How do I know that you're ... real?' he stammered. The question was beneath contempt, so Michael didn't bother to reply.

'Look,' continued Gideon, 'if you *are* the Lord, then I should offer you a present, so just wait while I do a little experiment.' That's another thing you must know about Earthlings. They're so proud of their intellects that they have to try to explain everything scientifically.[35] If they can't produce 'proof' of the supernatural, they prefer to say it doesn't exist. The more intelligent the Earthling, the less likely he is to believe in our existence. There was a little French Earthling once, a peasant girl called Joan of Arc. A group of Messengers was sent down to her while she was out working in the fields one day. Like Gideon, she was told to free her nation from occupation – which she did with a great deal of help from us. No one had any trouble believing that a mere peasant girl could do an impossible thing like that, but when she started talking about angels and saying *we* had helped, they burnt her alive as a witch! Terrible, but when you have the chance to meet her, you'll find that her reward up here is so enormous that she hardly remembers the incident now at all.

Gideon was a born sceptic too, but he knew from his Granny's stories that the Mighty One is always pleased when someone gives Him the most precious thing they have – as a sacred offering. So off he ran, to find what was definitely most precious in a land blighted by famine – food. He cooked up the best meal he could and rushed it back to the oak tree, all laid out in his Mum's best crockery.

'If he eats it,' he told himself, 'then I'll know he's only some hungry old tramp, playing tricks.' He laid the meal out on top of a big, flat stone, and Michael reached out his walking stick and, as it touched the food, fire came out of the rock and the whole thing went up in smoke – including Mother's best clay pot! The Angel himself stepped into the flames and rose with them, until he disappeared from Gideon's view.

Well, an experience like that changes a man for life! Gideon fought some amazing battles, sent the invaders packing, and then set about purging the entire land. Gideon turned out to be a great reformer, but he was always a worrier – that never changed. The Mighty One often had to do little miracles to keep his fears at bay.[36]

*

We angels have come to realize that the Mighty One often uses frightened Earthlings simply because their fears make them cling to Him all the harder. And my next story proves that point nicely. The central character this time was never afraid of anything, and that was his downfall. He lived hundreds of years after Gideon, and once again the Jews had reneged on their pact with the Mighty One, and were suffering for it. This time they had been overrun by a mean lot called the Philistines. This Earthling was called Samson, and his life also revolved around a visit from Michael.

Notes

1. Josh. 1:1–2.
2. Num. 13:33, AV.
3. Num. 33:50–56.
4. Josh. 5:11–12.
5. Josh. 5:13–15.
6. Heb. 1:3–9.
7. Josh. 6:1–5.
8. Judg. 1:27–36.
9. Judg. 2:1.
10. Judg. 2:10.
11. Isa. 38:15–17.
12. Prov. 30:8–9.
13. Judg. 2:20; 3:6.
14. Ps. 106:34–39; 2 Kings 14:23.
15. Prov. 14:12, *The Message*.
16. Judg. 2:12–13.
17. Ps. 106:40–42.
18. Job 7:20.
19. 2 Kings 17:17.

20. 1 John 4:20.
21. Lev. 5:5–6.
22. Luke 15:3–7.
23. Rev. 21:27.
24. Judg. 3:9.
25. Neh. 2:4–5.
26. Ps. 103:1–2.
27. Rev. 8:3.
28. Acts 16:22–26.
29. Matt. 5:14–16.
30. Eph. 6:11–12.
31. Mark 16:17.
32. John 14:12.
33. Luke 8:31; Rev. 17:8.
34. Judg. 6:1–6.
35. Job 6:24–26.
36. Judg. 8 – 9.

Chapter 6

An Earthling King

Samson's parents, who were both Lighted Ones, had a nice little farm in the fertile plain not far from the spot where Sodom had once stood.[1] In fact, they lived in the village where the two angels took Lot and his daughters for safety, that terrible day when disaster struck the cities on the plain. Farmer Manoah and his wife were doing very well for themselves, but to their great sorrow they had no son to work the land after them. We sometimes feel so sad for childless Earthlings. Their longing to hold a baby can be so intense, and yet up here in Heaven we have so many babies and tiny children. They each have their own angel to play with them, hold them close and rock them to sleep in their arms. They are the Earthling babies who die before they are old enough to be given the gift of choice. Many of them died because they were unwanted or neglected, and some of the tiniest ones were even murdered by their parents before they had the chance to be born.

Beware of another Earthling absurdity. These little ones who reach Heaven as babies do *not* turn into angels. Earthlings love to think they do, but angels and humans were created separately and are totally different beings. People *never* become angels and angels *never* become people. Earthlings often like to say, 'Oh yes, I believe in angels. My next-door neighbour was a real angel to me when I was ill.' Ridiculous! Humans can be kind – even unlighted ones – but they are never 'angels'. That kind of talk is a real insult to us!

As I was saying, we feel sad for those childless Earthlings who would give all they possess for one of our heavenly babies. But, of course, it would be unthinkable to send a baby down to Earth – they are so very much happier up here where there is no pain, tears, loneliness or rejection.[2] The Mighty One Himself is a Father to them, and angels make far better mothers than even the most maternal human being.

One day Mrs Manoah was busy in her kitchen when someone knocked at the door. On the threshold stood Michael. His back was to the sun, and all she could see was a shining silhouette, but her heart beat very fast indeed.

'I have a message for you from God,' began Michael. Remember, angels never waste time with small talk! 'You've never been able to have children, but you will soon have a son. He will be a special child, adopted by God from birth. As a sign that he is highly favoured he must never cut his hair or drink alcohol. You, too, must refrain from everything to do with the grapevine while you are pregnant. Your child will rescue this land from the Philistines.'

Speechless with astonishment, the woman ran out to the fields to tell her husband. You might have thought he'd be pleased, but not a bit of it. He was thoroughly cross. His masculine pride was badly dented because God had sent the message to his wife instead of talking directly to him.

'Silly woman!' he snapped. 'You're imagining things.' Then curiosity got the better of him and he added, 'What was this messenger like, anyway?'

Mrs Manoah arranged her comfortable bulk on the nearest boulder and replied thoughtfully, 'At first I thought he was one of those wandering prophets – you know, the preachers who stand in marketplaces trying to turn people back to Yahweh, but I think he was actually ... an angel.'

'Now I *know* you're going senile!' sneered Manoah, and he stalked off to spread muck on his fields. But, while he worked, tears of rage pricked his eyes.

'Silly woman,' he kept muttering. 'Angels, indeed! No one believes in angels these days. But just suppose ...?'

He often prayed as he worked, and that's why the Mighty One could trust him with a special child – silly little man though he undoubtedly was! Leaning on his staff, knee-deep in dung, he prayed, 'Please, Lord, let that travelling prophet come and talk to me too – that's if he exists at all!'

At that very moment his wife's fat, round figure appeared, running at full tilt from the melon field.

'He's back!' she panted as she wiped the sweat from her nose with the corner of her apron. Manoah flung down his fork and ran as if a large bull were after him.

'If it *was* an angel,' he thought, 'it'll have disappeared by the time I get there.'

He arrived long before his wife, but there was only one person in the melon field – an elderly stranger, leaning over the gate with his back towards the farmer.

'Excuse me,' puffed Manoah. 'Are you the gent who's been speaking to my wife?'

'Yes,' replied Michael without turning round. Manoah didn't quite know what to say next, so he stood scratching his bald head rather awkwardly.

'Well, then,' he managed at last, 'when this boy's safely born, what are we supposed to *do* with him?'

'I've already told your wife,' was the calm reply.

'Yes, but ... she's only a woman,' replied Manoah, pulling himself up and brushing the straw from his tunic.

Of course, up here in Heaven there is no difference between male and female, black or white, old or young; all are equally precious. But, sadly, it's never been like that down on Earth.[3] There they tend to underestimate the female of the species quite dreadfully. Some women can be very stupid, of course – you'll soon discover that – but in the main they are more susceptible to us angels, and to the Mighty One Himself, than their menfolk are.[4] Many of them see us angels, but when they try to tell men about us, their stories are dismissed as 'female fancy'.

Michael patiently repeated the instructions he had already given to Manoah's wife, while the farmer listened with his mouth hanging open in amazement. He was still sure this was no angel, but common courtesy decreed that any visitor should be well fed, so as soon as his wife panted up, Manoah sent her off again to cook a meal.

'You mark my words, Manoah,' she said. 'He won't eat it – he'll burn it up, just like that old story about Gideon's angel.'

'Nonsense,' retorted her husband.

'Well, I'm not going to put the meal on my nice dining-table,' she declared. 'I don't want a hole burnt right in the middle of it, now do I?' So they compromised, and set the stranger's meal on a rock in a shady corner of their back garden. It was the family altar where they had often sacrificed lambs for their sins. As Manoah conducted the stranger to the feast, he was feeling increasingly uncomfortable. There was something about the way the man's skin shone, and his clothes were just too white to be real. A nasty idea crossed Manoah's mind. Suppose his wife was right after all?

'What's your name?' he asked abruptly. 'We'd like to know, so when our son is born we can call him after you, and perhaps invite you to be guest of honour at his circumcision.'

'My name is too wonderful for Earthlings like you to know,' was the reply and, as the angel looked Manoah straight in the eye, the farmer *knew* for sure that he owed his wife an apology.

'Oh, Sir, s-s-stay with us,' he stammered, but Michael shook his head and, as fire from Heaven licked up the meal, once again he disappeared in the flames.

'We'll die now for sure!' cried Manoah. His wife gave him a withering look.

'Why should God kill us when he's taken so much trouble to tell us that we're going to have a child?' Her blistering logic finally silenced the farmer's doubts for good.

Now you'll notice another classic Earthling reaction which I've already warned you about. That man wanted to get onto first-name terms – to make friends – even to keep the angel like a domesticated house cow. Watch out for that – women who see angels can even fall in love with them, and start all kinds of silly fantasies. I've said it before, but I'll say it again – the Mighty One made Earthlings for Himself, to be His friends, not ours. And He won't tolerate our stealing their love.

In due course Mr and Mrs Manoah had a baby boy, and they called him Samson. A hefty great lad he was, too! He was known as the strongest man who ever lived. The Mighty

One used that phenomenal strength to get rid of the Philistines.[5] But it was his strength that was Samson's undoing. He didn't have to rely on the Mighty One like poor little Gideon. I suppose he was so strong and successful that he felt he did not need help from above. In the end he became so vain that he even thought he was above keeping the Mighty One's Ten Rules, and he got into all kinds of trouble with women. Eventually the Warrior Angels, who had secretly been the cause of his success, were called off protection duty, so that he was soon caught by the Philistines. They gouged out his eyes and locked him up in a dungeon. The Mighty One can't abide pride because it destroys that dependence and trust which go hand in hand with the love He craves. That's why He enjoys using the weak, the ordinary and the ignorant – because their love isn't tainted by self-confidence.

Angels can hardly credit the cruelty of tearing out someone's eyes, and leaving them, without medical treatment, in blindness and agony. Poor Samson! But he wasn't alone – the Mighty One was just waiting for him to call for help, and a great sigh of relief swept round Heaven when he finally did.

Angels were despatched instantly to comfort him, and Messenger Angels used constant thought-planting to keep his hope alive. Soon he 'just knew' that God would use him again one day, even though the idea didn't seem humanly likely. One day 3,000 Philistines got together for a huge party. For entertainment they had Samson brought in so that they could mock his weakness. Many of the Philistine warriors had embarrassing memories of meeting him on battlefields, so they really had it in for him.

Right in the middle of that jeering, taunting rabble of drunks Samson looked up into the Mighty One's face and whispered, 'Give me back my strength, just one more time.' Instantly, in response to his look of faith, we were commanded to help him. Two Watcher Angels had spotted that the roof and galleries of the building were supported entirely by two huge stone pillars. Each angel took one of Samson's hands and guided them to these pillars, which, because of his blindness, he did not realize were there. Then a Senior Angel who was standing behind him touched Samson on the head and sent a huge surge of strength right through his body. Gripping both pillars, he did the humanly impossible – he pulled them towards one another, snapping them in half. Of course, the whole building collapsed, killing the 3,000 Philistines in one go. It was a magnificent military triumph for Samson, even though he did not stay on Earth to be congratulated. The angels surrounding him quickly scooped his spirit out of the falling rubble and transported him up here to enjoy a far greater reward.

By the way, that is something that we angels do find hard to take. Samson had failed and let the Mighty One down badly; yet all he had to do, in his dungeon, was repent and, to the Mighty One, it was just as if he had never sinned at all![6] Angels just have to accept that Love delights in forgiving lavishly.[7]

✱

Now, you may well think it's strange, but the human who loved the Mighty One more than anyone else (in our opinion) only saw an angel on one occasion in his life – and that was so dreadful that he certainly could have done without it! His name was David – King David. He was always aware of our presence, though, and often mentioned us in his songs.[8]

When he was in a tight spot on the battlefield, he often used to say he felt angels camping all round him,[9] and he certainly wouldn't have survived all his desperate adventures if we *hadn't* been there with him.

How that man loved making music for the Mighty One! Until his day, worshipping through songs was thought to be women's stuff – too soft for men. David didn't care – he had to express his love somehow, and the Mighty One *revelled* in it. Nothing makes Him happier than when the people He loves start to worship Him. We angels love it too, and we're always attracted to Earth when a group of humans begin to worship. We cluster in their churches, sitting on the window-ledges, perching on the rafters or standing on the backs of the pews. We'll even straddle the church roof or balance on top of the steeple, just so long as we sing with them, and play our instruments in harmony with theirs. Lighted Ones are never so safe from the enemy as when they are worshipping the Mighty One with all their hearts.[10]

David introduced choirs and orchestras, and organized a whole programme of worship far more wonderful than any cathedral they've got down there on Earth now. Sometimes he just had to dance for joy – he couldn't stop himself – and we angels danced with him.[11]

David seemed to love everyone he met – men, women and even the disabled, who were usually ignored in those days.[12] Because the Mighty One is Love, He seems to value that quality most of all in His Lighted Ones, and He nicknamed David 'the man after my own heart'.[13]

Being that precious to the Mighty One made David a number-one target for the enemy. They watched him for years, but he never gave them a chance to move in close. His continuous attitude of worship and love excluded them completely, but then, one day they had him at last!

You'll find that the Others aren't particularly creative in their work. They use the same old strategies over and over again, because they find that they always work well with humans. First they'll try to break a Lighted One's line of communication with the Mighty One – stop him praying or going to worship with others.[14] Then, they'll try to make him depend on himself – figure out ways of solving his own problems rather than relying on the Mighty One for His wisdom.[15] Once they've messed up a Lighted One's friendship with God, their next objective is to lower their victim's resistance levels by encouraging overwork or laziness. Then, finally, they're ready to cause a massive breakage of the Ten Rules of Happiness. They'll dangle the seamier pleasures of Earth in front of our poor charge's eyes, like a fisherman baiting a hook with a lovely juicy worm.[16]

It's our job to protect our Earthlings, but it's so frustrating because sometimes they just don't want to be protected – they like sinning too much.[17] We are left feeling remarkably helpless, considering how powerful angels are!

One awful spring[18] they actually succeeded in taking David through all these stages until at last, from the roof of his palace, he caught sight of a pretty girl taking a bath. That sort of thing leaves us angels cold – we see it millions of times every day, and it gets boring after a while. But the dark angels on David's case were clever – they certainly knew his weak spot. Our hearts sank (or they would have, if we *had* hearts) when we overheard the message that a dirty little demon was signalling back to satanic headquarters:

'See excellent chance to nobble D comma who's fancying

An Earthling King

someone else's wife stop await instructions stop please advise immediately stop'

Lucifer's answer came back instantly: 'Try Lie Number 5 and keep me posted stop'

By the way, Lucifer's Lot are just as good at thought-planting as we are, but they do have one huge disadvantage – their commander can't read human minds and ours can. He is extremely limited, for all his big talk, but his agents have remarkable powers of observation, and they can read human body language and facial expressions so well that their guesses are usually accurate.

Lie 5 is one of Lucifer's favourites and his agent planted it at once:

'God loves you so much that He'll understand if you break His Rules – just this once. After all, He wants you to be happy, doesn't He?' The lie worked for the same reason that it *always* does – it was exactly what David *wanted* to hear, and in a surprisingly short time the girl was in his bed.

At this stage I must warn you how agonizing it is for us angels to watch our charges being defeated by Lucifer's Lot. We have to stand by and watch all the sordid details, when we feel like crashing in there and shaking some sense into our charge before it's all too late. Of course, we can't, thanks to that much vaunted gift of choice! To us it feels like having to watch a mangy old cat grabbing the wing of a beautiful bird, and bringing it down into the dirt and dust, trapped and no longer able to fly free. Poor, stupid David! And it wasn't long before he had stooped to lies and murder to cover his tracks. How could it have happened? The Mighty One sat and wept. We could only try to imagine the agony that such rejection caused Him. When ordinary Earthlings kill and

101

wrong each other it always gets to Him, but when His special Lighted Ones let Him down it causes him the most intense pain.[19] Lucifer *loves* doing that to Him – that's why he concentrates all his effort on snuffing out the Lights.

For months it looked as if David was going to get away with it; he even married the girl after he'd had her soldier husband conveniently killed in battle. But the Mighty One didn't have His eyes shut; He was just too hurt to speak for a while.

Yes? I see a wing in the air. You, over on my right?

Good question, that. When the light is quenched, does the name in the Great Book also have to be rubbed out, barring the Lighted One's entry into Heaven at the point of death?

Firstly, don't go falling into the Earthling trap of assuming that the worst sins are adultery and murder. No, it's not sins like that which snuff out spirit lights, it's pride. Pride was the first sin,[20] and it's also the worst, because a proud person becomes so sure of himself that he stops relying on the Mighty One. He can't see any of his own failings and so he feels no need to say sorry, and it is only by repentance that his light can be lit again.[21]

The Mighty One, being Love, always goes on hoping to the very end that they will turn back to Him, and always sends an angel to give them one last chance of re-ignition just before they leave their body. Some of these last-ditch attempts are successful, but we do know that the Mighty One often cries over that book when He's all on His own. So perhaps it's the blank spaces He's grieving over.[22] Only He knows that.

Anyway,[23] after many months of silence the Mighty One only had to send David a message, via another Earthling, pointing out that He was upset, and such was David's love for his Maker that he collapsed in a tearful heap. He cried for hours, and tears of repentance never fail to melt the Almighty's heart. David was soon safely covered again by the mantle of grace,[24] and Lucifer was extremely angry – he *hates* repentance!

David's other lapse was a bit more painful all round, and it was on that occasion that he saw the terrible Angel of Death.[25] David had been a brilliantly successful king for many years, when Lucifer decided to launch another major attack.[26] 'You've ruled these people really well,' a senior Fallen Angel thought-planted one day. 'Look how their numbers have increased during all these years of peace that your military skills have won for them. It might be interesting to know just how many fighting-men you have at your disposal. Then you'd feel really safe. After all, you never know when those Philistines will make another invasion plan.' Census-taking was a 'no-no' with the Mighty One, because He wanted His people to rely on *Him*, and not put their trust in military power. David's servants reminded him of that, but Lucifer had said what David wanted to hear, and it was easy for the Others to play on his pride and desire for independence.

'Just get on and do as you're told,' David ordered his advisers. When all the counting was done and he was gloating over the sheer size of his own importance the Mighty One sent down one of His Special Squad Angels (Earthlings call them 'conscience'). They carry sharp-ended sticks, and their job is to prick Earthlings in the heart.[27]

'My conscience smote me,' Earthlings say, and never realize that it was an angel poking them all the time. David shed yet more tears of repentance, and the Mighty One gave him a choice of punishment. He could choose three years of famine and starvation for the nation, three months of enemy defeats, or three days with the Angel of Death let loose in the land with his dreaded plagues.[28] David shook in his royal shoes, because he knew that whichever he chose, his stupidity was going to cause terrible suffering.

'Punish me by your Angel, Sir,' he said at last, 'because I know you are merciful.'

I don't suppose you'll ever see the Angel of Death himself. He keeps out of the way up here most of the time, and very few Earthlings have ever seen him either. He's the largest of all the Angels of Judgement. He has seven officers who each carry a bowl.[29] These are full of germs, viruses, diseases, disasters and plagues which the Angel of Death blows over cities, and even whole nations, causing widespread illness and death. They're a grim lot, those Angels of Judgement – I wouldn't want their job. Lucifer likes to make Earthlings think that they don't exist.

'There's no such thing as Hell or punishment to come.' That's his Lie Number 9, and Number 10 adds, 'Everyone will get to Heaven one day – God couldn't possibly banish His creatures.'[30] But real Love isn't weak like that. Whenever one of those Ten Rules of Happiness is broken, someone else gets hurt. It's the innocent who are usually the victims of greed and selfishness, and the Mighty One can't ignore their cries of pain.[31] As Ruler of the Universe, He can't let people get away with hurting others just because He's too soft to punish them. If they went scot-free there'd soon be anarchy, and no one would be safe. Laws are meaningless without a penalty for those who break them, and that's why He has to have Angels of Judgement. Oh yes, they exist all right, whatever Lucifer likes to pretend.

Anyway, they began blowing those plague viruses all over the Land, and David was horrified at how many people they killed – 70,000 in all.[32]

'Bring out your dead!' was the cry of the mass grave-diggers, as they trailed through the streets of every town.

By the end of two days the plague was spreading towards the brand-new city of Jerusalem, travelling at high speed. David stood on the city wall that evening, so upset that he didn't know what to do with himself. It was dusk, but the housewives were not lighting the lamps in the little houses, and the stew-pots were cold and empty on the dead ashes in the hearths. A terrible atmosphere of doom hung like a heavy blanket over the rooftops. Children cried dismally, and somewhere a lone dog began to howl.

Everyone knew the plague was coming and they didn't want to die. A menacing presence caused David to look up towards the evening star. It was then that he saw the Angel of Death, hovering over the highest point of the hill, just outside the city. The Angel was so gigantic that he filled the sky between Earth and Heaven as he stood motionless between the two worlds. His sword held poised over the city, at any minute he would give the order for his seven officers to uncover their deadly bowls and waft their contents onto the evening breeze.[33]

'Oh no!' sobbed poor David. 'It's all my fault! Let me die, instead of these poor, innocent people. Put your sword through my heart instead.' (He truly was a man after God's own heart!) Instantly the Mighty One dismissed His Angel, and David crumpled onto the ground in sheer relief.

Later, David went to the farmer who owned the spot where the Angel of Death had stopped and the city was spared. He bought the land and built an altar, and offered hundreds of valuable sacrifices there. The greater the sin, the more precious is the sacrifice that will pay for it. That spot was always used after that as a sacred place, and the great Temple of Jerusalem was later built there.

Most of the time, David was one of the happiest men who ever lived, but he shed a lot of tears, too. Perhaps that is why the Mighty One let him into a very special secret. He explained to David about the bottles of tears that we have up here in Heaven.[34] I haven't told you about them yet, have I? There is a quiet room not far from the Mighty One's throne. The walls are covered with shelves on which are rows of bottles – big ones, small ones, some very old and others new and unused. Each is carefully labelled with an Earthling's name. Sometimes in the lonely darkness down there they shed broken-hearted tears. They think no one is watching and no one cares. But, of course, when they are Lighted Ones, the Mighty One cares intensely and sends particularly gentle angels down to collect the teardrops and carry them on the palms of their hands, infinitely carefully, to present to the Mighty One Himself. He minds so very much, you see. In fact, He gets so involved that He sometimes adds His own tears to theirs.[35]

You may well be thinking, 'If He minds so much, why does He allow them to suffer at all?' He'd save them from everything unpleasant, if only He could, but, during the very brief speck of time that they spend down there in Lucifer's province, He is limited by another of the gifts He gave them – the right to be human. Humans are always getting hurt – it's normal for them. If He put them in cotton wool He'd take away their humanness and make them into robots – a bit like us, I suppose. But these natural human events are exactly what cause the tears. Even though the Mighty One knows they'll be safe from all suffering soon – when they get up here – He still hates to see them cry, even for a moment. So the tears they shed are infinitely precious to Him. He Himself slides the tears safely into the bottle which already bears the correct name. No angel has ever been considered worthy to do the decanting for Him – not even the great Cherubim themselves. But the angels who work in that department are allowed to replace the bottle in its own space on the shelf. Working in the Tear Room is a job of the highest possible prestige.

Angels still talk about the grandeur of David's reception celebration when he finally died and was carried safely up here to join us. His son, the most intelligent man who ever lived, was crowned in his place, and it was this Solomon who built the great Temple round the spot where the Angel of Death had been halted.[36] By human standards it was a very grand building, one of the seven wonders of the world, but we angels had to laugh – as if the majesty of the Mighty One could ever be contained in any wobbly little structure built by Earthlings! But the Mighty One seemed pleased with it.[37]

✱

After David and Solomon many kings ruled the Mighty One's people. Some had lighted flames and helped the people to stay close to Him. Others were full of darkness and dragged the people back into Baal worship which, of course, brought the Angels of Judgement swiftly down on all their heads.[38]

After David's time no Messenger Angels actually appeared on the Earth for many years. The Mighty One talked to his people through men called Prophets.[39] He hoped that humans would find it easier to realize that He loved them if another human being told them so.

These Prophets are friends of His who have mastered the art of hearing His voice, and are brave enough to warn lesser mortals of the dangers of disobedience. But how the Prophets have suffered for their courage! Earthlings, who haven't liked the Mighty One's messages, threw stones at them; beat them with whips;[40] threw them into prison; chucked them down wells[41] and even cut them in half.[42] They needed us angels to cheer them up, I can tell you.

Sometimes we were sent down to them with instructions and messages,[43] but often these men and women heard the Mighty One for themselves. Their main job was to hand on His messages to other Earthlings, and the things they said were so precious to Him that He began to have them compiled into the book which men now call the Bible. He used some of the jottings that Moses had made on stone slabs to start off His book,[44] added some of David's poetry, Solomon's wise little sayings and some very long, depressing warnings from other people too. He also recorded the exploits of many famous Lighted Ones, so that other Earthlings could learn from their experiences.[45] He even put in some stories about us. The whole book took Him more than a thousand years to write, and He used many different secretaries to take down all His dictation.[46]

'Why is He so busy making this book for Earthlings?' some of us asked Gabriel one day.

'He'll use it as a way of communicating with them,' replied Gabriel.

'But surely ... He uses us for that!'[47] I must confess, we felt a bit upset. 'Is He trying to make us redundant or something?'

Gabriel threw back his head and laughed at us.

'The Mighty One knows how bound Earthlings are by their material world. He's always telling us that most of them only believe in things they can experience with their five senses.[48] So He's giving them His messages in a book they can touch, see, smell and even hear, when it's being read aloud. Seeing

His messages in black and white will be safer than just hearing them from us, because humans so easily forget or distort our spoken words. But don't worry,' he added kindly, 'His Majesty will still need Messenger Angels to remind Earthlings to read His book, to open it in the right place for them, and even to underline the words they need to read.'

And that is exactly what we do – many times a day. How we laugh when an Earthling tells his friends, 'The words jumped right off the page! It felt exactly as if God was talking to me personally!' Well, of course He was! Another trick of ours is to dredge up words from the Bible out of the Earthling's memory, and then flash them into his conscious mind, just when he's least expecting it. He'll probably say, 'I didn't know I knew that was even in the Bible!' Yes, Messenger Angels have to move with the times, like everyone else in the universe.

But I was in the middle of telling you how we were used to help the Prophets, wasn't I?

Notes

1. Judg. 13:1–2.
2. Rev 7:17; 21:4.
3. Gal. 3:27–29.
4. Luke 24:1–11.
5. Judg. 24 – 26.
6. Luke 15:18–24.
7. 1 Cor. 13:4–8.
8. Ps. 34:7; 35:5–6; 103:20.
9. Ps. 34:7.
10. 2 Chron. 20:21–22.
11. 2 Sam. 6:5.

12. 2 Sam. 9:3–7.
13. Acts 13:22.
14. Heb. 10:25.
15. Jer. 2:13.
16. James 1:14–15.
17. Job 21:14–15; John 3:19.
18. 2 Sam. 11:1.
19. Isa. 5:1–4.
20. Committed by Lucifer.
21. Jer. 15:19.
22. Rev. 3:5.
23. 2 Sam. 12:1–13.
24. Isa. 61:10.
25. 1 Chron. 21:1–26.
26. 1 Chron. 21:1.
27. Acts 9:5, AV.
28. Rev. 15:1.
29. Rev. 15:7.
30. Gen. 3:4.
31. Gen. 4:10–12.
32. 2 Sam. 24:15.
33. Rev. 15:6–8.
34. Ps. 56:8, AV.
35. John 11:35.
36. 1 Kings 6:1–38.
37. Isa. 11:1.
38. 2 Kings 21:1–18.
39. Heb. 1:1.
40. Jer. 20:2.
41. Jer. 38:6.
42. Heb. 11:37.
43. 2 Kings 1:15.

44. Exod. 24:4.
45. 2 Tim. 3:16–17.
46. Heb. 2:2–3.
47. Zech. 1:12–15.
48. John 20:25.

Chapter 7

Plans for the Lighted Ones

One of our favourite Prophets was the shaggy-haired wild-man Elijah.[1] He had the court manners of a mountain billy-goat, and the royal family loathed him. They had publicly decreed that Yahweh no longer existed and only Baal should be worshipped. So naturally, they were furious when Elijah delivered a message from the 'non-existent' Creator of the Universe, saying it wouldn't rain again until *He* said so! King Ahab and Queen Jezebel were so angry that Elijah had to make a hasty run for it and hide in the mountains, where he would certainly have died of hunger if several of us hadn't been told to assume the shape of ravens and carry food to him twice a day. Later we provided a starving widow with an endless supply of grain and oil to share with him. You see, there is absolutely nothing we can't do, so long as our charges have the faith to depend on the Mighty One for all their needs.

Plans for the Lighted Ones

Later the same Prophet, Elijah, was running for his life yet again,[2] this time from wicked Queen Jezebel herself. Poor Elijah was stressed out after a huge attempt to swing the nation back to the Mighty One[3] and, when the Queen vowed that she'd wipe him out, he reached the end of his rope. We were horrified when we saw him dashing off into the wilderness at dead of night, considering what a huge celestial bodyguard he'd been given for his personal protection. Why, the angels who surrounded Elijah outnumbered the Queen's palace guards ten to one – *and* they were all ten times taller! But Elijah was just too discouraged to realize that, and he finally collapsed under a tree in the desert, not far from that famous wadi where the slave-girl Hagar had rested.

'I've had enough,' we heard him say. 'I want to die.'

Even his Guardian appearing in front of him in full glory didn't cheer him up; poor Elijah was just too tired. He simply forced down the food that the angel cooked for him and went back to sleep. (Yes, we angels can cook, and practical demonstrations will be given later in the course.)

Next day the angel woke him up again and made him swallow more food. 'Eat up,' he said. 'You're going on a long journey and you need lots of energy.'

'I don't want to go anywhere,' mumbled Elijah. 'I just want to die. God's people have broken their side of the bargain that He made with them on Mount Sinai, back in the days of Moses. They have turned away from Him and I can't convince them to turn back again, however hard I try. I'm the only one left who still loves Him.'

The angel smiled at him, because he could see something that Elijah was too depressed to notice. There were at least 7,000 other Lights still burning in the Land of Israel.[4]

'You need to go to Mount Sinai, where it all began,' Elijah's Guardian told him through a thought-plant. 'Perhaps the Mighty One will even speak to you there and encourage you a bit. You've lost your sense of proportion, that's all.'

Of course, Elijah didn't realize that he was being addressed by an angel – he just thought he was having some very good ideas all of a sudden. So he sank back into sleep, vowing that he'd set off for Sinai at first light. But Sinai was 40 days' walk away, over some of the meanest stretches of desert on Earth. That man was suffering from extreme nervous exhaustion; he was far too ill to stagger more than a few steps. So all night long, as Elijah slept, his Guardian sat next to him with a hand on his shoulder, allowing the healing power of Heaven to flow into his charge. Next morning Elijah bounced up, so full of energy that he didn't even wait for breakfast.

There's another important lesson for you in that story. We angels call the job which Elijah's Guardian did that night 'imparting heavenly strength'. When an Earthling is ill or exhausted, and a prayer missile is launched on their behalf, the Mighty One gives us permission to minister healing to that Earthling. You simply put a hand on his head or shoulder and your being becomes a conduit pipe, conveying the healing power of Heaven straight into your charge. The Earthling never knows it's happening, of course, but one of their Prophets once said, 'They that wait on the Lord shall renew their strength.'[5] In other words, resting in the presence of the Mighty One and trusting Him entirely makes it possible for Him to use us angels in this way. An even better method is to encourage other Earthlings to minister with you.[6] Get them to lay their hands on the patient, and then you put your hand on them; combined, you make an even more powerful conduit pipe, and the Earthlings have the joy of feeling that they are being used by the Mighty One, which builds faith like nothing else!

Obviously, Elijah's angel had no other Earthlings to call on, since he was stuck out there in the desert. You'll probably all face similar situations on Earth. You'll soon discover that this kind of heavenly strengthening is part of your daily, routine work.

We do use other methods of healing on rare occasions. In Jerusalem, the city that David built, there was a pool called Bethesda.[7] Once a year one of us was sent down to inject the water with heavenly healing power, and the first Earthling who stepped in was always healed. There have been other incidents like that, when we've been allowed to touch wells or springs, and healing miracles have resulted.[8]

Sometimes we are despatched by the Mighty One to help surgeons with complicated operations and repair jobs. The only problem with that method is that the Earthling gets all the credit for our hard work! But we don't mind – it's our charge who matters!

So Elijah set off to walk for 40 days across the desert, still mentally patting himself on the back for thinking up such a good plan. The great Mount Sinai, which he had heard so much about, shook with earthquakes, raged with fierce fires and was whipped by howling gales, just as it had been when Moses and all the people of Israel were there so long before.[9] Elijah, huddled in a cave near the summit, finally heard a gentle whisper speaking kindly to him, and he knew that God had come to restore his vision. He went back to work again with fresh vigour and, before we were sent to fetch him home, disguised as chariots of fire,[10] he had managed to turn the people back to God most successfully – with a few visible interventions from us angels to help him![11]

Elijah's friend and assistant Elisha was also a very susceptible Lighted One and was very aware of us and our activities.
During his time on Earth the Jews were being bullied by the
king of Syria, and we angels had such fun with him! One of
us would be sent to sit in on all the meetings that the Syrian
king had with his generals, and then the angel would relay
their battle plans to Elisha by a simple thought-plant. Off
Elisha would run to the king of Israel, and 'mysteriously' his
armies were able to avoid every ambush and prepare in
advance for the fierce attacks which were designed to take
them by surprise. Of course, the angel *could* have gone
directly to the king, but, as I'm always telling you, pitifully
few of those humans are susceptible enough for that kind of
direct intervention.

The Syrians came to the conclusion that they were up
against a vast network of spies, and their informants named
Elisha as the main espionage agent.

'*Get him!*' ordered the Syrian king, 'and bring him here
alive! With intelligence like his, I could conquer the entire
world!'

His soldiers set off at once, and it didn't take crack troops
like them very long to corner Elisha in a small fortified town
called Dothan. They were armed to the teeth and well
equipped with the latest war chariots and teams of highly
trained military horses. They reached Dothan late one dark
night and silently surrounded the city, waiting to jump the
gates at first light. Elisha knew they were there – he could
hear harnesses jangling and the rattling of bits – but he also
knew all about Warrior Angels, so he calmly went to sleep.
His young servant was not so well up in spiritual warfare.

When he peeped over the city wall in the grey light of dawn, he was terrified and hastily shook his master awake.

'We're doomed, sir!' he shrieked. 'What shall we do?'

'Nothing,' yawned Elisha, pulling his blanket back over his head. 'There are far more on our side than there are on theirs.'[12]

'But that's just it, sir – there isn't anyone on our side!' sobbed the boy. 'None of the king's soldiers are here to protect us. We're doomed, I tell you!'

'Lord,' Elisha prayed with a sleepy sigh, 'open his eyes and let him see. Then perhaps I can get some sleep!' His prayer was answered promptly, and when the boy looked again he saw the surrounding hillsides covered completely with horses and chariots of fire, ridden by massive Warrior Angels, in armour which glittered in the light of the rising sun.

Elisha hardly had time to drop back to sleep before the Syrians attacked the main gate of the city with blood-curdling war-cries and a great deal of sword waving.

'Strike those noisy men blind, Lord,' said Elisha without taking his head from under the blanket.

'Master, Master!' shouted the boy an hour later. 'All those soldiers are groping about the city streets and falling over each other. Come and see them, quick!'

With a sigh Elisha put on his sandals and followed the boy to the city gates.

'You're in the wrong place, lads,' he said. 'You won't find your man here. I'll lead you to him, if you like.'

Those soldiers were trained never to fail so, in spite of their horrendous handicap, they felt their way to their horses, mounted and doggedly followed the sound of Elisha's voice. He took them all the way to his king in the royal city of Samaria and right in through the gateway of the royal fortress. Jewish soldiers ran from every direction to surround them, and *how* we enjoyed the look of astonishment on their faces when they realized that none of their prisoners could see a thing! Then Elisha prayed once again.

'Open their eyes, Lord,' and instantly all the Syrian commandos saw *exactly* where they were!

'Shall I kill them, Elisha?' lisped the king.

'Idiot,' muttered Elisha under his breath. 'Certainly not, your Majesty,' he said out loud. 'Give them a good meal and send them home to their king. The disgrace will be a worse punishment than death.'

Yes, it really is a great treat for us angels when we're allowed to intervene in Earth situations like that. But wouldn't you think that when that kind of thing happened, to help a king whip his enemies, all the rulers who came after him would be sure to follow the Mighty One closely? Well, Earthling minds don't seem to work like that! They're born sceptics and, just as they never believe a fisherman about the size of his catch, they're just as easily able to dismiss true stories of angels and miracles. As the years went by, there seemed to be far more kings who wanted to worship Lucifer than the Mighty One.

So, watching the Jews blowing all their chances of world influence was pretty depressing for us angels, when you remember how much help we *could* have given them, if only they'd obeyed the Mighty One.

But I can see your wings drooping with discouragement and, believe me, I wish I could be telling you a different story, but that gift of choice has given everyone so much trouble! The Mighty One could do absolutely anything in the universe He had created – every living creature was entirely in his power – but He was helplessly unable to do the one thing he wanted to do most, and that was to *make* those Earthlings return His love. His perfect love gave them perfect freedom. If, before the Mighty One had first created mankind, we angels had known just how very few of them would ever choose to love and obey Him, surely we could have done something to save Him from being hurt so badly.[13] We find it so hard to see His pain as He watches all the needless suffering that they bring on themselves and their innocent little children. Perhaps it's just as well that angels weren't created to know the future, just to serve.

Of course, the Mighty One *can* see into the future, only too clearly. He knew how it would be but, like I told you, He's willing to go through the grief that the vast majority give Him simply for the joy that He gets from the love of a few. That's another reason, I suppose, why those few are so incredibly important while they live on Earth. If only they could grasp even a tiny measure of their own value to the Mighty One, and to all of us up here in Heaven, what a difference it would make to them while they live in the gloom down there!

Now, although many Prophets saw angels, very few were ever allowed to see the Seraphim or Cherubim. One of the lucky ones was a man called Isaiah. He was worshipping one day in the Temple which Solomon had built in Jerusalem when he saw right into Heaven.[14] There was the Mighty One on His Great Throne, and He seemed to fill the entire Temple. You should have seen the poor lad's expression as he watched the Seraphim circling round Him and heard the sound of their praise. The noise of their wings is almost deafening to human ears, and so much light radiates from them that Earth-eyes can be blinded.[15]

The sheer holiness of the Mighty One got to the young man, and he realized, as all Earthlings do when they come near Him, just what a sinner he was, and he cried out in an agony of repentance. He'd always had a problem with bad language, you see, and suddenly he hated himself for it. The Mighty One sent one of the Seraphs over to the Temple brazier to fetch a red-hot coal to put on Isaiah's lips. He was badly burnt, and his face was scarred and disfigured for life. To those of us who watched, it seemed a bit cruel, but we later realized how important that young man's words were to become in the history of the Earth. The book he later wrote has ignited the spirits of so many Earthlings,[16] and he communicates the heart of the Mighty One so beautifully that, naturally, his mouth had to be sterilized thoroughly if his words were to be pure.

As Isaiah stood there, shaking with terror, he heard the Mighty One sharing with some of His senior Seraphim how desperately sad He felt about His people. 'Who'll go and tell them how much I love them?' He asked sadly.

'I'll go!' shouted Isaiah, interrupting the heavenly board meeting in his enthusiasm. The Mighty One *loves* that kind of thing, so the boy was commissioned as a Prophet on the spot. He suffered for it, of course, just as all the Prophets do, but now that he's safely up here, he certainly reckons it was all worth it.

There have been several of the Mighty One's Prophets who have been allowed to see into our world and to hear us talking to each other, as Isaiah did that day.[17] One was an older man, Ezekiel;[18] then there were the Prophets Micaiah[19] and Zechariah;[20] a royal prince called Daniel;[21] and later in time,

Stephen,[22] Paul[23] and John.[24] Now, it's not only the Earthlings that I've mentioned who have paid us a visit up here during their Earth-times. They are well known because their accounts were all recorded in the Mighty One's Great Book. But there have been thousands of obscure Lighted Ones who loved the Mighty One so much that He couldn't resist inviting them up here for a short visit, just to have a look round. When they talk about it later, other Earthlings shut them up in mental hospitals or simply ignore their stories. We angels love showing them around; and that's a nice little job that you can look forward to, once you've got a bit of experience.

Well, in spite of the preaching of great Prophets like Isaiah, the Jews still wanted to do their own thing (as Lucifer would say). It was during the reign of one of the worst kings of all that our angelic patience finally snapped. The sight of an altar to Baal (Lucifer himself) in the Lord's Temple finally did it. Black magic and the occult were the 'in thing', and King Manasseh even offered his own children to Lucifer in the ghastly Valley of Death just outside Jerusalem.[25] Fortune-tellers, mediums and wizards were so fashionable that they made themselves fabulously wealthy. All the same old, disgusting stuff was back, with added virulence. The King broke every one of the Ten Rules of Happiness and boasted that he *enjoyed* doing so.

Naturally, the misery down there in Israel was enormous – bullies ruled society and even grabbed the food out of the mouths of widows and orphans. Talk about loving others as much as themselves! The stench of their selfishness used to waft up here to Heaven, and it would have turned our stomachs if angels *had* stomachs to turn!

The Mighty One's great idea of using the Jews as an object lesson just was not working.[26] His plans had gone sadly wrong. We were all getting so upset for the Mighty One that Michael, Gabriel and several leading Cherubim went to see Him. The rest of us gathered round at a respectful distance, but we were all listening carefully to see what would happen. Michael, who always takes the lead at times like that, spoke up for us all.

'Highest King of the Universe,' he began, after the usual 'Holy, Holy, Holy' intro. 'I come to make a deep apology. I have failed abysmally in my task. You put me in charge of your people the Jews,[27] commanding me to keep them safe from evil attacks, but these people will not be protected. They prefer to listen to Lucifer's agents than to my angels. None of us can go on seeing you looking so heartbroken over the spoiling of the wonderful plans you had for your people. They simply are not making any progress with their assignment; in fact, the only kind of love they are displaying to the rest of the world is their love for themselves![28]

'Greatest Sovereign, surely the time has come for you to put an end to the pain you are suffering. Send me and my Warriors, together with the mighty Reaper Angels, and we will clean up the whole Earth for you – rid the universe of mankind forever. Or, if that seems too drastic, we will confine ourselves to the destruction of the people of Israel and drive them out of their Land, just as you sent Cherubim to put Adam and Eve out of the Garden of Eden.'[29]

After a long and awkward silence, the Mighty One replied heavily, 'The Jews will have to be driven out of their Land, and their cities must be reduced to ruins, but there is no need for your angels to do such an upsetting job. I have already appointed the Emperor of Babylon to do it for me.[30] He will burn Jerusalem to the ground, pulling down the city walls and destroying the lovely Temple that Solomon built so carefully for me. Then he will drag away all my people to be his slaves in Babylon.'

A sigh rippled round Heaven. We were so relieved. At long last He'd seen sense.

'Your Majestic Highness,' said Michael, 'these people have broken their side of the bargain that You made with them. They deserve to perish for ever.'

'Oh no!' replied the Mighty One hastily. 'That's not the way it's going to end. I haven't finished with them yet!' His words caused a gasp of astonishment this time. 'After 70 years I will call them back to Jerusalem so that they can rebuild it all.'[31]

'But Gracious One,' protested Michael, 'surely you realize that they will soon turn away from You yet again? Why not cut Your losses and forget that You ever chose them?'

'I could never do that,' was the sad reply. 'I love them,[32] their very names are tattooed on the palms of my hands.[33] And anyway, I promised my friend Abraham, and his son and grandson,[34] that I would bless every nation in the world through their descendants. And that has not yet happened.'

'But Sire, the gift of choice you gave those Earthlings constantly works against your plans. You must see that.'

Michael was being very daring that day. Some of us even thought he had reached the point of audacity.

'Glorious Master, these people won't listen to the Prophets, to the words of Your Great Book or to Messenger Angels.[35] Surely they won't ever change, even after 70 years of slavery. Please, Great All-Knowing One, try to hear what your angels are saying.'

There was such a long silence that we covered our faces hurriedly and said a few quick 'Holy, Holy, Holies' as loudly as we dared. We all dread the Mighty One's anger – but when

He spoke again there was a smile in His voice and we breathed a sigh of relief.

'I can see that I must let you angels into my secret,' He said at last. 'You are right – My people will not listen to the Prophets or to My Book. But My plan has always been to step down into their world Myself one day, to show them My love in person.'

'Gracious One,' gasped Michael, 'You surely are not planning to leave us all here *alone* in Heaven?'

The Mighty One laughed out loud. 'How can God leave Heaven?' He said. 'No, I can be both there and here at the same time – surely you know that! I am omnipresent, but your angel minds find that concept hard to grasp. Because Earthlings have the same difficulty, it will be easier for them to call the part of Me which is seen on Earth 'the Son of God'. But because I am one God, it will be Me, Myself, who goes to Earth – I, the One who created the world and by whose authority the universe hangs together.[36] When they see the part of Me that they will call My Son, they will see Me; when they know Him, they will also know Me, and they will understand once and for all what I am like.'

The meeting ended abruptly as we angels exploded with joy. Cheers, shouts of praise and great waves of applause went on for so long that even the Seraphim and Cherubim grew hoarse.

'What a brilliant idea!' we all told one another. He was going *Himself*! If the Mighty One went down there in person and Earthlings could *see* Him as we angels see Him, in all His glory, then they would all fall down before Him, covering their faces and saying, 'Holy, Holy, Holy,' just as we do. Abraham, King David and all the hundreds of Prophets may have failed to show the rest of the world what He is like, but *He* could not fail if He went Himself. Soon all humans would love Him and happiness would cover the whole Earth! (Well, that's what we thought!)

✲

The surge of excitement that we felt after that Heavenly Assembly really helped us angels through the next difficult years. We had to watch some grizzly sights on Earth, I can tell you. Jerusalem, David's great city, was gutted by the Babylonians, and not one stone of Solomon's beautiful Temple was left on another. Emperor Nebuchadnezzar didn't spare the rest of the Jewish cities either. The mess was indescribable – everything valuable was stolen, including, of course, all the beautiful utensils used to worship the Mighty One in His Temple.[37]

Even worse was the plunder of people. All the Jews were dragged away, chained in great columns of human suffering. The only people left were the old, the disabled and the insane. They camped among the ruins until they were picked off by roving gangs of squatters who soon settled the land. What an outrage! The beautiful valleys, plains and farmlands that were given to Abraham were taken over by Lucifer-lovers who had no right to be there at all. And we angels weren't even allowed to kick them out!

There was one old man left, wandering heartbroken among the blackened stones that had once been Jerusalem – he was an old Prophet called Jeremiah. We were all overjoyed when one night a Messenger Angel was allowed to administer a thought-plant (or, because it was a very important one, it should really be called a prophecy) in his mind. He was told to send a letter to the Jewish slaves in Babylon, telling them that the Mighty One had not forgotten them; His plans were to bring them prosperity and hope for the future.[38] He was also told to tell them that in 70 years' time they would be allowed home.

That letter had the most remarkable effect on the Jewish exiles (or, at least, on those who were susceptible enough to believe the old Prophet's words). 'We can put up with life here so long as we know we're going back one day,' they told each other.

In Babylon the Jews had no Temple to worship in, but we were told to encourage each of the scattered communities to build themselves little places where they could meet to pray and worship regularly. They called them synagogues, and they most certainly helped to keep up national morale. The Jews really did return to the Mighty One in their hearts, as so often happens during adversity, and they did their best to keep His Rules of Happiness.

On the Sabbath days, when they met together, it was our job to plant their minds with hope and courage; and we were greatly helped by Earthlings like Ezra, who travelled from synagogue to synagogue teaching people from the Mighty One's Great Book.

By the way, that kind of regular, once-a-week meeting for Lighted Ones is absolutely vital for their well-being. Praying, worshipping and being inspired through the Book, together in a group, has a quite remarkable effect. Because they each bring their own angels to the meeting with them, just think how many angels are concentrated together when you have a hundred Lighted Ones grouped in one place! The spiritual power that's generated is colossal and, of course, when they separate again the Lighted Ones go away feeling empowered and encouraged to face another week. They call them churches down there on Earth these days, and each one of them has its own angel in charge.

We were also helped in our job of encouragement by a Prophet called Ezekiel. He was allowed to see into Heaven on a number of occasions, and he was given detailed plans for the new Temple that would one day be built in Jerusalem.[39] When he travelled round the synagogues telling people that he'd seen Cherubim and the glorious, dazzling splendour of the Mighty One's presence,[40] excitement began to run high. The Jews worked so hard that they soon prospered in Babylon and began successful businesses, but they were careful to keep separate from the Babylonians in order to maintain their national identity.

The Mighty One had arranged that four young princes should catch the Emperor's eye, and they were sent by him to the best university in Babylon.[41] They were all most susceptible to the supernatural, and some of their experiences have been well documented. For instance, three of them had a very near shave once, when the Emperor's power went to his head and he decided that he was a god. Making a huge image of himself, he commanded everyone to bow down and worship it – which, of course, no Lighted Jew could possibly do.[42] When he caught sight of these three princes standing up straight, when everyone else had their heads on the floor, he screamed with rage and threatened to have them flung into a nearby metal-smelting furnace.

'If your god's real, he'll save you!' he sneered, but Shadrach, Meshach and Abednego looked at him coolly and said, 'Our God is able to deliver us, but even if He doesn't choose to, we're still going to worship Him and Him alone.'

Into the furnace they went, and the heat was so intense that the soldiers who pushed them in died on the spot – but not Shadrach, Meshach and Abednego! There in the flames with them was Michael himself, sent to take care of them; and the Emperor actually saw him there. Nebuchadnezzar was so terrified that he had the fire doused at once, and the princes were pulled out, with not so much as a singe mark on them!

A few years later, Daniel, the other prince, was thrown into a pit full of hungry lions, and he should have been torn to pieces before he hit the stone floor, but an angel was sent to shut their mouths. The prince used the biggest lion as a pillow and slept peacefully all night.[43]

This same Daniel became a highly respected politician in the Persian government, because the Mighty One had given him a remarkably well-developed gift of wisdom. Towards the end of his long life he was asleep one night when the Mighty One allowed his spirit to rise into Heaven.[44] He saw far into the future, right to the Great Day of Judgement when all the Books are opened wide.[45] Earthlings hate to think about that day, but Lighted Ones who have been forgiven have nothing to fear – though it will be a frightful experience for ordinary humans, I'm afraid![46]

Daniel saw things that night which certainly rattled him immensely. You don't need to know the details at this stage but, while I'm on the subject of the Books, I think I should mention the Recording Angel. He posts his angelic division all over the Earth,[47] one to each Earthling, and their job is to record everything which happens to that individual and their every word and action. When a Lighted One finally arrives up here, and he's had a chance to spend time with the Mighty One, he is allowed to see the Recording Angel's records. People used to describe these records as Books, but nowadays Earthlings would probably think of them as more like a video film. One of us goes through it with him, before the great day when the Mighty One Himself will open all the records Himself.[48] Each Lighted One, on average, has six million hours on Earth; some get far less and some get more, but it works out at about the six-million mark. Many of those Lighted Ones are horrified, when they have their session with the Recording Angel, to find out just how *few* of those six million hours they spent with the One they so glibly called 'Lord'. We have clergy, monks and nuns, of course, who look a bit smug at first, imagining that they are going to be patted on the head for all those cold hours they spent kneeling or chanting in church and cloister. But some discover, to their dismay, that many of those hours were no joy to the Mighty One, because their hearts were so full of bitterness, greed, lustful thoughts or worldly plans that they were not really praying at all. They were just going through an outward act to impress other humans. Often it is the harassed mothers, dashing through their action-packed days, or the missionary doctors and nurses, faced with a daily stream of suffering patients, who seem to learn the art of communicating with the Mighty One inside their busy activity.

Some Lighted Ones get very agitated at the thought of the Recording Angel and his records. They remember all the horrible sins they have committed and wonder how they are going to face having them all revealed in Heaven. What they don't seem to realize is that when the Mighty One forgives He also chooses to forget, and the whole sequence is deleted from their records instantly.[49] That's why some of the Recording Angel's records are very short;[50] the Lighted One had to ask forgiveness for so many bad things that there was precious little left to show for all his years on Earth.

You'll probably hear Earthlings say that Heaven is full of human beings who've been good all their lives. Ridiculous! Heaven's full of humans who were bad, and knew they were bad, but asked the Mighty One to do something about it! Yes, forgiveness is a mystery to us – but then, angels weren't created to be forgiven, just to serve.

Notes

1. 1 Kings 17:1.
2. 1 Kings 19:1–3.
3. 1 Kings 18:18–46.
4. 1 Kings 19:18.
5. Isa. 40:31.
6. Acts 9:17–18.
7. John 5:4.
8. There are many well-documented examples in Church history.
9. 1 Kings 19:9–18; Exod. 19:18.
10. 2 Kings 1:3, 15.
11. 2 Kings 1:3.
12. 2 Kings 6:16.
13. Jer. 2:32.
14. Isa. 6:1–13.
15. Acts 9:3, 8.
16. Acts 8:28–35.
17. 2 Chron. 18:18.
18. Ezek 1:1–28.
19. 2 Chron. 18:18.
20. Zech. 3:1–10.
21. Dan. 10:1–21.
22. Acts 7:55–56.
23. 2 Cor. 12:2–4.

24. Rev. 1:9.
25. 2 Chron. 33:1–9.
26. Isa. 49:6.
27. Dan. 12:1.
28. Isa. 1:23.
29. Gen. 3:23–24.
30. Jer. 20:4–5.
31. Dan. 9:1–2.
32. Jer. 31:3.
33. Isa. 49:16.
34. Gen. 22:15–18.
35. Luke 16:27–31.
36. John 14:9–10; Heb. 1:1–3.
37. 2 Kings 24 – 25.
38. Jer. 29:11.
39. Ezek. 40 – 43.
40. Ezek. 1:1–28.
41. Dan. 1:1–7.
42. Dan. 3:1–27.
43. Dan. 6:22.
44. Dan. 7:1–10.
45. Rev. 20:12.
46. Matt. 25:31–46.
47. Zech. 1:8–11.
48. Matt. 12:36–37.
49. 1 John 1:9; Ps. 103:3.
50. Isa. 43:25.

Chapter 8

Angels
Astonished

There was another time when Daniel met Gabriel himself. He was reading the Mighty One's Book, late one
night, and he also had a copy of the letter that Jeremiah
had written to the exiles years before. Suddenly Daniel realized that those 70 years were just about up! (He was nearly
90 years old himself by that time.) The old man was suddenly gripped by a deep burden of prayer, and he fell on his
knees and began to repent of all the sins that his people, the
Jews, had committed against the Mighty One. His weeping
could be heard all over Heaven. And, of course, the Mighty
One just can't resist that kind of thing, so He beckoned
Gabriel and sent him flying down to Daniel to tell the old
statesman that Jerusalem would soon be rebuilt, with fine
streets and a brand-new Temple.

It was no surprise to us that after that, Daniel decided to
go away with a few friends to pray and fast for the Jewish

nation.[1] He realized that it was going to take a supernatural miracle to get them safely back to their own land, so for three weeks that dear old man prayed his heart out!

Then suddenly he saw a mighty angel approaching him through the clouds. He shone dazzling white and gold, and the sound of his voice was like a great storm at sea. The other men who were with Daniel were so terrified that they ran for their lives.

'Don't be afraid, Daniel,' he was told. 'God heard you the very first day you began to pray, and I was despatched to bring you the answer. But before I could reach you, the dark angel who rules Persia ambushed me and we fought a great battle. He is immensely powerful, and I would have been beaten completely if the Archangel Michael himself had not come to help me. Here I am, at last, with the answer to your prayer.'

Then the great angel told Daniel many things about the future of the Jewish nation – things that were hard for the old man to hear, and harder still for other Earthlings to understand, once he had written them all down. Then, finally, the angel said, 'I must leave you now and go and fight that dark prince of Persia once again. Michael will help me. The Jewish nation is his responsibility: he is their Guardian Angel and constantly fights the powers of darkness on their behalf.'[2] With that he left the old man and went off to do battle.

A lot of fierce warfare had to go on in the skies above the Earth during the following few years. Naturally, the very last thing that Lucifer's Lot wanted was for the Jews to go home and become a nation again. Their plan was for them to sink into oblivion, mingling comfortably with the cosmopolitan people who made up the province of Persia. But miraculously, and almost unbelievably, Michael and his Warriors got a group of Jews back across the thousands of miles of bandit-infested desert, carrying with them all the Temple valuables and a mass of treasure sent by the Jews who preferred to stay in Babylon.[3]

When they did reach Israel they had to deal with the squatters, who were far from pleased to give up their new homes. The Jewish settlers had so much rubbish and rubble to clear[4] that it made us angels tired just watching them (that is, if angels *could* get tired). To us, the Jews looked like agitated ants swarming over the pathetic heap of scattered stones. But the Temple was finally rebuilt[5] and, after a lot of skirmishes with the enemy – both the spiritual sort and the human sort – the walls of Jerusalem were completed. The nation was established once again, and they really did seem to stick a bit closer to the Mighty One – for a few centuries, anyway.

✷

It's a bit difficult for a mere working-class angel like me to tell you the next part of the story. You see, *now*, with hindsight, I can see the answers to so many of the questions that totally bewildered us angels at a time when so many important things were happening on Earth.

Right from the days of Isaiah, the young man with the burnt lips, the Mighty One kept on instructing his Prophets to tell the Jews that He was coming to live with them soon.[6] They were expecting their 'Messiah' to appear at any minute, and excitement was high. We angels were excited, too, at the wonderful thought of the Mighty One stepping down into the world He had made. We used to sit on the clouds discussing how humans would be affected by the sudden sight of His Majestic splendour – and how cross Lucifer and his Lot were going to be.

But time went by – centuries, to be accurate – and still nothing happened. We peeped anxiously through our feathers at the Mighty One's face but, as usual, He seemed to know what He was doing, although we certainly did not. Even when the Earth began to be threatened by a new world power called the Roman Empire, the Mighty One did not seem at all disturbed. These heathens worshipped Lucifer by many strange imaginary names, and laughed at the concept of one God who created the entire universe. But their soldiers were so well organized that Rome soon ruled the world, and even Israel was overrun by them.

'Never mind,' said the Jews, 'our Messiah will soon be here to deliver us from this tyranny,' and, just for once, we angels agreed with them!

Then, one day, the Mighty One beckoned Gabriel to His Great Throne and a buzz of expectancy shot round Heaven. Like I said before, Gabriel always gets all the plumb jobs, so we guessed that The Time had come at long last. In an atmosphere of tense excitement the Mighty One bent forward to instruct Gabriel. The rest of us were somewhat crestfallen because He spoke so softly that we could not hear a word he said. Gabriel's expression was also hard to read as he prepared for his mission to Earth. No disguise for him that day – he was to appear in full angelic glory and, as he sped through the gates, I have to admit that he looked very glorious indeed. You'll have guessed that we were all at the windows of Heaven craning our necks to see where he went.

'Yes, that's most fitting,' we all said with a sigh of satisfaction when we saw him alight on the highest pinnacle of the Temple in Jerusalem. Obviously Gabriel had been instructed to proclaim the Messiah's imminent arrival to all the faithful Jews who were worshipping there, and we waited in tense silence to hear the grandeur of his voice. But Gabriel was only resting, composing himself for his big moment.

A very old priest was on duty in the Holy Place of the Temple that day, offering incense in front of the Golden Altar.[7] When Gabriel finally stepped through the roof, it was to this old man alone that he showed his glory – the great crowds of worshippers in the outer courts of the Temple saw nothing unusual at all.

The priest was a Lighted One of high spiritual rank, but we all knew that a great cloud of grief had been hanging over him for many years. He and his elderly wife had no children. He was such a shaky old man that we couldn't help wondering why Gabriel had been sent to *him*.

Typically, he was terrified when he caught sight of an angel, standing in the flickering light of the giant candles. We wondered if the shock would kill him. He didn't look much better even when Gabriel started with our usual conversation opener, 'Fear not!' Gabriel continued, 'your prayer has been heard; and you and your wife will soon have a baby son whose name will be John. He will be a Prophet like Elijah, and his mission in life will be to tell people to get ready for their Messiah.'

And do you know what? The old man didn't believe him! Yes, I'm afraid I'm not joking. Poor Gabriel – you should have seen his face! A priest, right in the Holy Place, insulting him like that!

'Look here,' the old man croaked in his wobbly voice, 'my wife and I are getting on a bit! Don't you think you just might have got this wrong? I don't want to get all excited only to find that you aren't speaking the truth.'

The sheer audacity of a mere Earthling talking like that to Gabriel, one of the seven greatest angels who were allowed to stand in the presence of God![8] We could all see that he was most upset. He pulled himself to his full height – which is considerable – and he looked all the way down at the wobbly geriatric in front of him; but the priest was still talking. Some Earthlings talk far too much when they are frightened.

'You see, I don't really believe in angels – people nowadays don't, you know. After all, nobody's ever seen one, not since the days of Daniel – centuries ago – and modern theologians feel that Daniel's stories were purely symbolic.'[9]

'I am Gabriel,' boomed the great angel in an awesome voice. 'I spend my time standing in the presence of God, who sent me to tell you this good news. But because you have not believed me, you will be unable to speak until your son is born.'

And without another word he glided back to Heaven, leaving the old priest hurrying out of the Holy Place, waving his arms and hopping up and down. The worshippers gazed at him in amazement, but, of course, he couldn't tell them what had happened.

'Well, things are moving at long last!' we told one another.

'Yes, that baby will be The Voice,' said a rather scholarly angel who loves reading books. 'The Prophet Isaiah said, long ago, that a messenger would be sent to get the Jews ready for the Mighty One's great appearance: "A voice cries out, Prepare in the wilderness a road for the Lord."'[10] We all nodded, trying to look as if we'd known about this all along.

'When He goes down there to Earth, in all His majesty, He'll need brand-new roads built in His honour.'

We were all happily anticipating the Royal Welcome when the scholarly angel dropped his bombshell.

'You do realize, don't you, that when the Mighty One steps down to Earth, He intends to go as a human baby.'

Dead silence greeted this distasteful remark. We were stunned. And then the irritation began to set in. Most of us found that particular angel a bit too smug, and even a shade stuck up, with all the reading that he does. Most of us have too much to do to have time to wade through all those endless Earthling books. But he was still talking:

'Isaiah says, and I quote, "Unto us a child is given."[11] And he also talks about a virgin becoming pregnant and then calling her baby "the God who is with us".[12] The birth is going to take place in David's home town, Bethlehem.[13] You lot should try doing a bit of reading, you really should.'

'B-b-but ... but He couldn't allow Himself to be *born* in that ghastly, messy, Earthling way!' we stammered in horror. 'Surely it's enough that He should step down to Earth at all – accompanied by flashing lights, thunderstorms and tidal waves, not to mention angel choirs and trumpeters.'

'Well,' persisted the Scholar Angel, 'it says here in black and white that He'll appear as a human baby.' Gabriel himself had been listening to our conversation, and I noticed that he looked profoundly shocked.

'When my Messengers were given those words to take to Isaiah, I assumed that it was poetic licence ...' His voice trailed away – he was quite overcome. 'A baby! Surely He wouldn't go to such extreme lengths as *that* to show His love for mankind?'

Gradually we began to take in the implications of all that the Scholarly Angel was saying. To become a baby, the Creator of the Universe would have to put *Himself* into the uterus of a woman! How could the infinitely large become so minutely small? And then go through that disgusting squeezing, squashing, heaving, pushing, bloody experience of human birth? How could the All-Powerful One become anything as ridiculously helpless as a human baby?

'Perhaps,' said Gabriel thoughtfully, 'this virgin whom the Prophet talks about will be a royal princess – the daughter of a noble line of royal kings. If the Mighty One is to be born in a great and beautiful palace, it might not be quite so terrible.'

During the next three months of Earth time, we working-class angels discussed, at length, the various palaces that were on offer down there, trying to decide which one we felt was magnificent enough for the greatest event in the history of the world. Frankly, we couldn't see a single one which we felt was remotely suitable.

'Perhaps the Mighty One will have one built especially – with golden walls, diamond windows and white marble floors. After all, he created the Garden of Eden especially for Adam and Eve.' That was my modest suggestion.

Then we began to consider the kind of princess who might be worthy of such an honour! We combed the whole Earth, sifting through all the major royal houses, and we even took a brief look at some lesser regal families – just in case. This particular princess would have to be flawless in character, beautiful in body and soul, and perfect in spirit. But, before we could find anyone approaching a suitable candidate, Gabriel was summoned to another of those infuriatingly secret briefing sessions.

'Which palace, which princess?' we all wondered, as once again we peered out through the heavenly windows. Gabriel missed the greatest palaces of China and India by thousands of miles, veered past the wonders of Rome and even ignored Herod's pathetic little palace in Jerusalem.

'Where *ever* is he going?' we muttered in consternation. Then, to our horror, we saw him alight on the roof of a small hovel – a very poor little place indeed, in an unimportant, North-country village.

'No self-respecting princess would be seen dead in a dump like that!'

Earthlings have many limitations, as you will have realized, and one of them is that their eyes can't see through barriers such as walls and roofs. It's just as well that angel vision isn't blocked by things like that. The rushes and dried camel droppings that roofed that little house did not prevent us from seeing just who Gabriel had gone to meet. You'll find it hard to believe this, but it was a mere peasant girl. She was about 15 years old, with rough, work-worn hands, a sunburnt face and wearing very ordinary, threadbare clothes – not even a string of beads to decorate her neck. But we could see the flame of her spirit, and we realized at once that she was a Lighted One of the highest possible rank.

'That explains it!' exclaimed the Guardian who was standing next to me. 'That Earthling girl has been allotted no less than 50 Angel Guardians ever since the day she was born. We could never understand, before, why she was considered to be so very important.'

Gabriel was obviously quite overcome by the immensity of the moment, and he even fluffed his usual opening line:

'Peace be with you,' he managed at last. 'The Lord God is with you and you are greatly blessed.' Although the girl was obviously one of those Earthlings who are perfectly at home with the supernatural, she did look rather overwhelmed by the extravagance of this greeting, so Gabriel's favourite opener fitted in quite comfortably at that point.

'Fear not!' he boomed more confidently, but as he went on to tell her that she would soon become pregnant, and bear a child called Jesus, who would reign forever and be called the Son of the Most High God, she began to look extremely worried. Clearing her throat apologetically, she whispered modestly, 'But Sir, I'm not actually married yet, so how ...?'

In what was, for him, a remarkably gentle voice, Gabriel said, 'The Spirit of the Mighty God will hover over you, and the power of the Highest One will overshadow you. Therefore the Holy Being whom you will eventually bear shall be called the Son of God. Go and visit your elderly cousin Elizabeth, the wife of that old priest Zechariah.' (Gabriel's voice became a little stiff at this point in the conversation.) 'You will find that she is six months pregnant, and that will convince you that there is nothing that God cannot do.'

Bless her, she responded magnificently then. She just bowed her lovely little head and she said, 'Let it happen as you say. I'm the Lord's servant. He can do whatever He likes with me.'

Oh, how I wish there were more Earthlings like her!

But later we saw how she cried – you see, she was so much in love with the local carpenter, a man called Joseph.[14] She was in the middle of sewing her wedding clothes and she wasn't at all sure how he would respond. Most single female Earthlings who get 'into trouble' try to think up an excuse to save their face, and sometimes their skin.[15] Saying she'd seen an angel was an old one – lots of people had tried that before. Engagements in those days were as binding as marriage, and the penalty for being unfaithful was death by stoning. Girls like that were tied up outside their father's front door and the injured party had the right to throw the first stone. So, for the first three months, her Guardian

Angels sweated (well, they would have, if angels could sweat). She was just so vulnerable!

We angels were not the only ones who had been watching Gabriel giving Mary the message. Lucifer's Lot had been there too, and they ran screaming all the way to their master with the bad news.[16]

Mary was in grave danger from that moment on, as millions of demon reinforcements were hurried from all over the universe to surround her. Of course, her own angelic bodyguard was increased massively,[17] but all the same ... it wasn't very nice to know that all those dark ones were watching everything she did or said. They were worried – very worried indeed – and reports came into Heaven constantly that their HQ was seething and bubbling with tension and demonic activity, with everyone held in a constant state of red alert. Lucifer was holding continuous cabinet meetings to discuss the situation and drawing up endless plans. Right from the beginning of time Lucifer had feared something like this; those words that the Mighty One had spoken to him in the Garden of Eden haunted him: 'A descendent of the woman will one day crush your head, and you will only be allowed to bruise his heel.'[18]

He knew he must destroy this child, preferably before it was even born. He was probably as surprised as we were that it was happening in such a simple way, but, of course, that played into his hands. A young, unmarried peasant girl would be easy to wipe out. But he was reckoning without us angels!

Travelling was a risky business in those days, especially for a girl on her own. To follow Gabriel's instructions meant that she had to leave the familiar hills of her home in the North and travel down to the sophisticated, street-wise world of the South. The main road was an international trade route, bustling with teams of donkeys, camel caravans, Roman legionaries, thieves, con men, and lonely business-men on the lookout for female company. She ignored them all – her mind was on other things! When an Earthling girl has just seen Gabriel in full ceremonial dress, nothing else on Earth is likely to frighten her; and she was turning over in her mind the implications of all that he had told her.

Her elderly cousin Elizabeth lived in a hilltop town not far from the capital city,[19] and it was easy for us to plant in Mary's mind the idea of making a detour and paying a visit to the Temple while she was so near.[20]

As she stood in the Women's Court, something happened which was more important than any previous event since mankind was created. As she stood there she began to wor-ship as I think I've hardly ever heard an Earthling worship before – or since. The praise just gushed out of her spirit like a waterfall after prolonged rain. She stood there with her arms lifted to Heaven, quite oblivious to the curious glances of onlookers. Tears streamed down her cheeks, and her face shone with love, as she communicated with the Mighty One in the deepest possible way. She may have been dressed in dull, dusty clothes, her face white with tiredness and her hair damp with the sweat of the journey, but at that moment she was more beautiful than any Earthling ever created. Or that's what we thought as we surrounded her on every side and stretched our wings over her to form a royal canopy.

Suddenly she grew quiet, gazing upwards with a look of rapt adoration on her face. A great stillness descended on the busy Temple Courtyard. We knew it was the presence of the Mighty One Himself hovering over her, and we bowed to the ground all around her. Mary stood alone in the middle of the heavenly circle, a gentle wind ruffling her hair and the corners of her cloak. Other worshippers in the courtyard stood still or sank to their knees. They had no idea what was happening, but all of them were aware of the pungent presence of Almighty God and the sweet scent of His personal fragrance.[21]

As we worshipped, our heads bent in adoration, a minute seed was planted in Mary's body. We had no words in Heaven to express the awe that we all felt when we realized what was happening. For that was the moment when the Mighty One Himself stepped down into the world of men.[22]

The thought is still too immense for angel minds to grasp. Suddenly we understood. Because the Mighty One so much wanted to be known intimately by the human beings He had made, and longed to identify with them in the smallness of their earthly lives, He had to become a human Himself. Before then they only knew Him as an abstract Spirit and, like I've already told you many times, Earthlings *have* to see with their eyes and hear with their ears and touch with their skins before they can believe that something exists. They would never be able to relate to the Mighty One until they could see His true character expressed by a human being like themselves.[23] They would never respond to His love until they saw it burning in the eyes of an ordinary man.

Mary and Elizabeth had a wonderful time together, and in spite of her great age, Elizabeth's baby was born safely. When all the local dignitaries arrived eight days later for the ceremony of circumcision, they were about to name the child Zechariah after his father. The old priest signalled for writing materials and, in large letters, he scrawled, 'His name is John'. Everyone was in the middle of protesting that no one in the family had ever been called John before, when an invisible angel touched his mouth and gave him back the gift of speech.

'He's called John because I was told by an angel to call him that!' exclaimed the old man. He had missed being able to speak so much that he was still talking when everyone else went to bed that night.

❋

As Mary trudged home up the main road towards the North country, she thought she was alone, but, of course, she had a larger escort surrounding her than any princess ever had. The humans who jostled against her on the busy thorough-fare where totally unaware of us, because, as spirits, we take up no space. You'll laugh when you first hear Earthlings arguing about how many angels can dance on the head of a pin. Ridiculous nonsense! But I suppose human minds are just too limited to understand a world beyond matter.

Naturally, we got her safely back home, even though we were aware of Lucifer's forces watching us from a safe dis-tance. Some were even masquerading as muggers or lecherous Roman soldiers, hoping to break through our guard. Unlike the humans, the Others could see us clearly and they knew they were not ready to launch an attack – just then. No, it wasn't until we got her back home in Nazareth that we hit our first big problem. When she broke the news to her fiancé, Joseph, that she was nearly three months pregnant he was horrified, and flatly refused to believe her story about Gabriel's visit.[24]

'Fool!' we all cried. He had been given the privilege of caring for the most favoured lady of all time!

My, that was a night that no angel will ever forget! It was terrible for us to watch her breaking her heart in her father's house while, down the street, Joseph paced up and down his carpenter's shop among the shavings and woodchips.

We kept on thinking about those cruel stones crushing her body – and the infinitely precious life it contained. Joseph couldn't bear the thought of those stones either – he really loved Mary, you see. Just as the first pink thread of dawn appeared in the east, he decided not to make a public fuss, but just to break off the engagement discreetly. We despaired as we heard him talking his thoughts out loud. We knew that, without his protection, Mary stood very little chance of survival. Once her condition began to show, she would be cast out of the close-knit community in deep disgrace. How would she and her baby survive then? Lucifer would soon be laughing all round the universe.

Notes

1. Dan. 10:1–21.
2. Dan. 10:13, 21; 12:1.
3. Ezra 1:6; 8:21–23.
4. Neh. 2:11–27.
5. Ezra 3:10–13; Neh. 4:11–13.
6. Isa. 11:1–5.
7. Luke 1:5–20.
8. Luke 1:19; Rev. 8:2.
9. Acts 23:8.
10. Isa. 40:3–5.
11. Isa. 9:6–7.
12. Isa. 7:14.
13. Micah 5:2.
14. Ps. 126:5–6.
15. John 8:3–7.
16. Job 1:7.
17. Ps. 5:11–12.

Angels Astonished

18. Gen. 3:15.
19. Luke 1:39.
20. We are not specifically told in the Bible that Mary did this.
21. 2 Cor. 2:14–16.
22. Mal. 3:1.
23. 2 Cor. 4:6.
24. Matt. 1:18–19.

Chapter 9

The High Prince to the Rescue

I t is hard to describe to you how frustrated we felt. The Mighty One Himself was existing inside that uterus. The hands that had formed the mountain ranges and poured water into the seas to make a play-pool for dolphins, the fingers that had put together bumblebee wings and precious stones deep in the rocks of the Earth, were now minute, hidden inside the belly of a peasant girl. The eyes that constantly watched every slight movement on Earth[1] and enjoyed the details of galaxies too far distant to be visible to any other being, were closed now in that small, dark hiding-place. And yet He was being rejected by the man ordained to be his earthly guardian. We were to discover over the next 33 years that He would often be rejected by the very people he had come to help – but that is another story.

It was almost time for Joseph to open the shop when he finally fell asleep, exhausted from wrestling with his emotions. But no sooner had his eyes shut at last, than Gabriel was unleashed to set the record straight – and how relieved we all were! Joseph had no more problems in believing Mary's story when Gabriel appeared before him in all his glory![2]

'Marry her at once,' were his orders – and he did! The wedding was a quiet affair on Earth, but it caused a tumultuous celebration in Heaven.

But, as time went on, we all became increasingly worried about the risks involved in the Mighty One being born in the mean little house behind the carpenter's shop. Mary kept it spotless, of course – she scrubbed the floor, polished everything each day and laundered the clothes most carefully, but … it was only a peasant's cottage. We angels knew all about the dangers of germs – we could see them long before Earthlings invented microscopes and discovered that they existed. Yet there didn't seem to be much that we could do about that, and we couldn't seem to stop the nasty, small-town gossip either. Spiteful faces watched Mary through cracks in the shutters, and nasty whispers followed her as she walked home from the village well.

'Look at her,' the other women would say. 'Only been married six months, but that baby's not waiting another three!'

We were incensed! How dare they call the Mother of the Mighty One rude names! Then, quite suddenly, we hit another unexpected problem.[3] Just when Mary ought to have been taking things really easy, those wretched Romans decided that she and Joseph must make a long, dangerous journey, 60 miles south, to the village of Bethlehem.

'I told you he'd be born in Bethlehem,' smiled the Scholarly Angel, but we all pretended we hadn't heard him. We watched in consternation as they packed their few possessions into a shabby saddlebag, strapped this onto their moth-eaten old donkey, and trudged off along the dusty road which led south.

We knew only too well just how many things can go wrong during the delivery of a first baby. At least one of us has been present at every birth that has ever taken place. Many a crestfallen Guardian Angel has had to carry his new charge home to Heaven before the tiny scrap has had a chance to make its first cry. Mary needed the comfort of her own familiar home about her at a time like this – however ordinary that little home might seem to us. By the end of that long journey she was tired, dusty and missing her mother badly.

The streets of the little town, where King David had once lived, were packed when they finally tried to push their way towards the inn, and already Mary knew that her pains had begun. We were all getting very flustered. Which house would they stay in? Would it be clean enough? The inn wasn't too bad, but we could see through the roof, so we knew that all the rooms were overcrowded already. So what next? Surely the part of the Mighty One who was still in Heaven controlling the universe would intervene now?

We watched, in gathering dismay, as Joseph banged on all the doors, but no one would let them in. There was no room in that dirty little place for the greatest King in all the Earth. It was David's town, but his greatest son was not wanted there.

'Talk about loving others as much as yourself,' we snorted. Surely someone would help a young woman in labour? In the end they were allowed to crawl into a cave where the animals were kept – a filthy, stinking place full of rats, spiders, chickens, goats and germs galore! The risk! Ruefully we remembered all those grand palaces that we had rejected as unworthy!

But Mary was a strong young woman, and her baby was born easily and without fuss. Just as we heard His voice raised in loud, and undeniably human, protest, we were summoned to the Great Throne.

'I want billions of you to celebrate this moment by filling the skies over Bethlehem.' Every angel who can sing or play an instrument is to be there – instantly. Sing all the songs of Heaven. Let the entire universe know what has happened in Bethlehem tonight.'

At last all that pent-up excitement and tension exploded in wave after wave of wonderful music. We wanted everyone in the town to hear the news, so we made as much noise as we possibly could. Our trumpet fanfares echoed round the sky, cymbals clashed and drums boomed. Heaven was almost deafened by our billion-voiced choir, but no one in that lousy little town heard us at all. They were down there in the mean little streets, busy eating, drinking, gossiping, making love, quarrelling about money and who slept with whom – totally Earthbound, not one of them had a spirit receptive enough to see our magnificent display. Really, these Earthlings do try our angelic patience!

And all the while the tiny baby snuggled up against His mother, and the mules and donkeys snored peacefully nearby.

All the same, there were just a few people who were sitting quietly enough to notice us – a group of shepherds. Well, I can see that the subtlety of that is lost on you, because you don't realize yet that shepherds were the lowest of the low down there. People said they smelt bad and must be idiots to spend their time with silly sheep. So they were the butt of every joke. It seemed a bit ironical that it was people like that who were the only ones to notice the most exuberant angelic performance ever staged! That's just typical of the Mighty One – to allow people whom Earthlings would deem the lowest of the low to see His glory first. These shepherds were sitting in the hills above the village, round their fire, when they noticed a strange light in the sky and heard us singing. When we'd calmed them down a bit, we sent them scurrying off to look for a baby in an animal feeding trough, and off they went, pounding towards the village at high speed.

It wasn't long before they found Him, and these rough men, despised by other people, were the first to worship the Mighty One in His human form. As they knelt in the dim lamplight, tears of wonder and joy rolled down their weatherworn faces and, as they reached out grimy fingers and tenderly touched His little head, the silence in that stable was awesome. Perhaps it was an act of worship more honouring than all our choirs of Heaven.

'His name's Jesus,' whispered Mary. 'An angel told me to call Him that; it means "Saviour". He's come to save people from their sins.'[5]

✷

In those days it was the custom for women to take 40 days' rest after childbirth,[6] to recuperate and bond with their babies. After that there was a cleansing ceremony in the Temple, and if the child was the first-born it was a special time of dedication too. It didn't seem worth going all those miles back to Nazareth, only to turn round and come back again for their Temple appearance. So Joseph found himself some casual work in the village, and eventually they moved into slightly more comfortable lodgings.

They were happy in Bethlehem and were almost beginning to wonder if they were supposed to stay there permanently. Somehow it seemed right to Mary and Joseph that this royal baby should grow up in David's town, but that was not the way it happened.

When the 40 days were completed, it didn't take them long to walk into Jerusalem early one morning. What a wonderful moment that was for us angels. We swarmed over the roofs and turrets of the Temple, and peeped round the pillars and marble archways. Here was Mary standing in the Court of Women yet again. Her clothes were even more shabby than when she had last been there. Her little child-like face had matured and already there were lines of suffering, invisible to Earthlings perhaps, but we could see them clearly.

But it was not Mary, this time, who absorbed our attention, but the tiny Being she held in her arms. The very One who had been worshipped here in this very spot for centuries. He had appeared in person – and no one noticed Him at all.

To all the people who bustled round them, preoccupied with their little self-important concerns, Mary and Joseph looked like a couple of nobodies, up from the country. Their baby appeared to be no more important than any other hungry brat. Yet we yearned to push back the windows of Heaven again and sing another great anthem, and tell those people to welcome and worship their Creator – but we were ordered to keep silent.

'Your High Majesty,' pleaded one of the Seven Leading Angels, '*Someone* must acknowledge this fantastic moment in history. Can't we notify the Chief Priest and Temple dignitaries, so that the High Prince of Heaven can be given the honour due to Him? Surely they would be delighted to know that their Messiah has come to them at last?'

The Mighty One had a strange expression on His face, which at the time we did not understand at all. He said, 'Sadly, they would *not* be delighted, and they would not believe it either, not even if *all* the angels in Heaven appeared at once. But I want some of you Messengers to go at once to two very special friends of mine and tell them to come and honour my Son. I have been preparing them for this moment for many years.'

We all expected these 'very special friends' to be leading members of the government, or even noblemen from Herod's household – but no, once again, we were dumb-founded by the Mighty One's choice. A little old man and a frail old woman came shuffling up to Mary and Joseph, led invisibly by the Messenger Angels.

'My prayers are answered at last!'' exclaimed the woman. 'I've been praying that the Messiah would come for these last 60 years.'

It's strange – Earthlings sometimes think it is *their* prayers which have galvanized the Mighty One into action. Actually, it works the other way round! When He decides that He wants to do something on Earth, He gives the spirit of a receptive Lighted One a little push and starts them praying for the very thing He intended to do in the first place. This is because, as I've already explained to you, He has decided only to act in conjunction with prayer. Don't ask me why – angels weren't created to be theologians, only to serve.

We do have to laugh, though, at those arrogant little humans who think prayer is a way of getting God to do what they want, when mostly it's a way of getting them to do what God wants!

Well, anyway, this old Prophetess called Anna had been living in the Temple for 60 years, praying for the Messiah to come, so she was sure that she was personally responsible for His arrival, and pottered happily off to tell everyone she met the fantastic news.

You'd have thought they would have all come flocking back to see the sight for themselves, but they thought she was just an old nutcase and completely ignored what she told them.

The old man was delighted too, but some of the things he said disturbed us angels a bit at the time. He took the baby in his arms and blessed all three of them. Nothing strange in that – it was the custom – but then he stood for a long time, looking at Mary's lovely face, smiling proudly down at her baby son. We later heard him say that he was 'seeing' the same face, but no longer young or smiling – a face etched by strain and twisted with agony, as she looked into that same son's face. For some reason that he could not understand, she was distraught, distressed beyond endurance.

'A sword will pierce your soul,' the old man said after a long pause, 'but the result will be the birth of honesty and truth.'[8]

I'm a bit ashamed to admit that most of us angels were of the opinion that this old man was a nutcase too, so we ignored what he said, just like the Earthlings.

Now, I feel there is one very important thing I ought to say. Just because I've told you this wonderful story in some detail, don't think that when you're a fully functioning angel you'll be able to see everything that's happening on Earth. We angels are allowed to watch from Heaven, but we can only focus on one situation at a time – unlike the Mighty One, who can see absolutely everything that goes on. All the same, we angels do know a lot because of the network of Watcher Angels stationed strategically throughout the universe. It is from them that we get our information. Angels can't see into the future, or read the thoughts of Earthlings either but, like the Fallen Angels, our powers of observation are extremely good.

So the young couple went back to their temporary home in Bethlehem and settled down to bring up baby Jesus. But even if His arrival on Earth had only been appreciated by a bunch of dusty, despised shepherds and a couple of old people, it was the one topic of conversation in Lucifer's headquarters. The Others certainly knew that He had arrived and, right from the start, they were plotting ways of getting rid of Him. Then a group of astrologers played into their hands by turning up in Jerusalem saying they had seen the magnificently bright star which announced the birth of the Greatest King in history.[9] They had been waiting for years to see the star, so naturally they came looking for the Royal Baby, even if it meant a journey which had taken them many months. They fell into the same trap as we had – thinking that He'd be born in a palace – but, obviously, it was a disaster when they turned up at the gates of Herod's residence in Jerusalem.

They gave the crafty old king the fright of his life.

'They've come to worship a baby king?' he spluttered, when his servants told him that the astrologers had arrived. The last thing that old fox wanted was someone coming along to take his crown off his head – he'd had enough of a struggle getting it there in the first place! He was so put out that he had to have several goblets of wine before he could face an audience with the visitors. While he was downing the fourth it was an easy matter for a demon to drop a cunning little thought-plant into his mind – though, of course, he thought the plan was his own brilliant statesmanship. He decided to sweet-talk the astrologers – get them to go and find the baby, then come back to tell him all about it, so he could deal with the situation – quickly.

'Messiah indeed!' we could hear him mutter. 'The Jews don't want a Messiah – we're part of the Roman Empire now, and independence would be very bad for trade.'[10] Lucifer even managed to convince him that he would be doing the best possible thing for the nation if he nipped this potentially dangerous affair in the bud.

So he sat himself down on his throne, in his best robes, and laid on a banquet fit to flatter even the wisest of wise men into a state of utter foolishness. We could scarcely believe our eyes when we saw them fall for it. Really, how stupid can Earthlings get? Herod dug up some ancient academic from a dusty Temple library, who found the same reference from the Old Book that our Scholarly Angel had also discovered.

'The great king you seek will be born in Bethlehem,' said Herod, sounding like a conjurer pulling a rabbit out of a hat. 'Go there at once and give him my deepest respects.'

You can imagine how we felt as we watched them setting out for Bethlehem. It wasn't even a comfort for us to see, at long last, some important-looking humans bowing down to the High Prince of Heaven and offering Him expensive gifts. Although we knew Lucifer was trying to use them for his own destructive purposes, we never for one moment thought that the High Prince of Heaven was in personal danger. It never entered our angel minds that He could be *killed*. No one can kill God – we were just distressed that all the heavenly plans were being disrupted.

'Greatest One,' pleaded Michael, 'please let me intervene,' and permission was granted. Those wise men were wiser than they seemed to us at first, and their leader was receptive enough to receive a dream-plant warning him about Herod. So they went home quickly by a route which avoided Jerusalem altogether. I only wish more Lighted Ones had sensitive spirits like that – protecting them would be so easy for us angels.[11]

Naturally, King Herod was furious when they didn't show up! He sent his soldiers marching off to Bethlehem at the double, to kill every baby boy under the age of two.[12] Only Lucifer himself could have thought up such a vile scheme. We angels have to watch the bloody massacres that he orchestrates far too often, but we never get used to them. The sheer ugly tragedy rises to Heaven like a ghastly stench.[13] You wait until you have to witness Earthling mothers weeping over the bodies of their dead children, and you'll discover that angels don't even have the relief of tears. But then, angels weren't created to grieve, just to serve.[14]

As the soldiers were on their way from Jerusalem, Gabriel himself was despatched to warn Joseph, and all three of them escaped just in time, and went back across the desert to that place called Egypt where we angels once caused so much havoc. There they stayed safely until Herod was dead and buried. Then they were sent another Messenger Angel who told them that they could go home to Nazareth.[15]

✣

Now I must confess that we ordinary, working-class angels were mystified as we watched that baby grow into a child. He was so completely human that it unnerved us! When He tumbled over and grazed His knee He bled, and because He felt pain, He cried – loudly – like any other Earthling child.[16] When He was hungry His stomach hurt and, again, He cried. To bleed, feel pain and then shed tears – these things never happen in Heaven, so it was astounding to us to see Him bound by Earth's limitations. He had a personal bodyguard of at least 10,000 angels,[17] so you might wonder how He came to fall over in the first place! But, you see, the Mighty One ordered us to keep our distance, because He must be allowed to grow up as any other human child.

'I have to allow pain for human beings, because without it the race could never survive,' He told us. 'Pain teaches Earthlings so many things.[18] Without it they would heedlessly damage the bodies I gave them; they would never learn obedience or know the tenderness of comforting love. My Son must not be like you angels, exempt from the discomforts of the world down there.'

I don't think we angels could ever quite understand that. To us it was so strange to see Him bound by His two feet, unable to glide through space, or across oceans and continents, as we can; unable to see through walls or closed doors, or hear voices further than the range of His human hearing. At first He did not even seem to know who He really was, and called Joseph 'Abba' (Daddy)! It did not begin to dawn on Him that He was not an ordinary boy, or that His real Father was Divine, until his Bar Mitzvah – His coming-of-age ceremony – when He was 12 years old.[19]

Yet, even with all these limitations, it was obvious that He was not the same as the boys with whom He played so happily. He was the most attractive human who ever lived. The laughter and joy that you've seen up here in Heaven was in Him; and wherever He went, Earthlings felt happy and safe.[20]

He had remarkable compassion too, even as a little boy – perhaps because He was not always absorbed by His own feelings and reactions, as Earthlings usually are. As He grew up, people often used to say how gentle He was and how sensitive He was to the needs of everyone around Him.

For 30 years He lived in the same ordinary little house behind the carpenter's shop, in the dull little village where people said nothing ever happened.[21] When Joseph died He took over the business and cared for His mother and her other children. These brothers and sisters found it hard to believe that He was more than a mere man. Mary did not talk about the strange details of His birth – she was a quiet woman who kept things to herself,[22] and perhaps she thought they might be jealous.[23]

As the years went by, we angels were beginning to wonder when He would 'show' Himself. He seemed content just to 'be' – He didn't *say* or *do* anything particularly noteworthy, except that He loved every single person whom He encountered in His shop or the marketplace, and bathed them in the peace of Heaven. Secretly, we angels felt that it would have been more fitting for the High Prince of Heaven to have lived like his cousin, John, the son of that toothless old priest who insulted Gabriel. John was a hermit, living alone in the wilderness, seeing no one and communing only with the Mighty One.[24] He did not have to spend his time with awkward customers or difficult neighbours. No lonely widows poured their woes into *his* ears, and children never brought their broken toys to *him* to be mended. He could enjoy being holy; and irritating Earthlings never ruffled the feathers of John's Guardian Angel.

When we told Gabriel how we felt, he roared with laughter. 'Surely you lot can see that, at long last, there's a human down there on Earth who's actually demonstrating *exactly* what the Mighty One has always wanted every Earthling to be like?'

We could see that he was right – Gabriel always is – but all the same, we might have felt a bit offended by that know-it-all attitude of his, if angels *could* feel offended.

'Look,' continued Gabriel more kindly, 'for 30 years now, the High Prince has lived in the light of the Mighty One's love and has returned that love with all the energy of His body, all the emotions of His heart, and with every thought in His head. He shows the same kind of unconditional love to everyone around Him, and that way He keeps the Ten Rules of Happiness effortlessly. He's never failed in one of them – not even once.'

'But doesn't He ever ... *want* to break one of the Rules?' asked a junior Messenger nervously.

'Of course He's tempted – He's entirely human and, as you can see, Lucifer's Lot keep firing thought-arrows[25] into His mind. But, if you watch Him, you'll see that He always pulls them out immediately and sends them back where they came from. If only Earthlings would realize that sin starts in the mind, when one of those arrows is allowed to stay until it's enjoyed. Lustful daydreams are as bad in the Mighty One's eyes as the act itself.[26] Anger and bitterness, which lead to hatred, are as much of a crime to Him as murder.'[27]

At that point Gabriel abruptly stopped talking, perhaps because he remembered that angels were not created to preach – just to serve!

✱

About the time when the High Prince of Heaven was 30, a great light suddenly burst into being down in the South of Israel, and a huge amount of spiritual activity was generated around it. The light came from the spirit of John, the hermit, who had exploded from his secluded desert and was being outrageously rude by the river Jordan. He called it preaching, but you could have said he was telling the leaders of the people exactly what everyone else wanted to say, but didn't dare! When smug religious Pharisees turned up, he told them they were nothing but snakes in the grass, and he gave soldiers and tax collectors a piece of his mind as well! The ordinary men in the street loved it, and hurried to the Jordan as fast as they could, hoping for more entertainment. But John didn't spare them either.

'Look,' he said, 'your Messiah is about to appear. Get yourselves ready – turn your backs on those sins that you think no one else knows about. Come on into the river with me and let me wash you clean from your filth.'[28] And in they went by the thousand. Soon, John was being discussed in every home, synagogue and back alley in the land.

'Perhaps he's the Messiah,' people speculated. We knew they were wrong, of course, but we couldn't help being excited. Gabriel had told John's father that his son would be the messenger sent before the Messiah to get people ready for His Royal entrance.

Right from babyhood, old Elizabeth had told John who his cousin Jesus *really* was, but he'd grown up with a terrible tendency to doubt (he took after his father!). The problem dogged him to the end of his life, and he needed constant reassurance from the Mighty One.[29] So, when he was still a lonely hermit, one of us had been sent with a message telling him that he would *know* for *sure* who the Messiah was when he saw a dove descend from an empty sky, and rest on the man he was baptizing.

How it amused us angels to see John squinting up into the sun above the head of any strong young man who stepped into the Jordan – looking for the dove from Heaven.

Then, one day, he spotted his cousin Jesus in the crowd. He had come with his family to Jordan, just like everyone else in Israel. We could see the awed expression on John's face, as he scrambled out of the muddy water to greet Jesus.

'Surely you ought to be baptising *me*,' he said, and didn't add, 'if you really *are* the Messiah.' But we could see several demons doubt-planting madly. The High Prince of Heaven held out His hand and laughed as He said, 'How else will you be really sure of my identity, cousin? We must do all that God requires.'

As He rose from the river, shaking the drops of water from His hair, not one of us was surprised to see the Spirit of the Mighty One gliding down in the shape of a dove and gently perching on His shoulder. John gazed in wonder, while Heaven vibrated with our cheers. Even the Mighty One Himself couldn't restrain His joy. His voice rose above the noise we were making and boomed out, 'You are my Son, chosen and marked by my love, delight of my life.'[30]

'Here He is, people of Israel!' cried John at the top of his voice. 'The One you have waited for is here at last!'

We could see that the crowd was impressed.

'Now He'll be carried on a tide of excitement up to Jerusalem,' we told each other, 'and there the religious leaders and members of parliament will worship Him – every one of them.'

But, like I said, we angels don't always get things right, and as soon as our cheering and dancing had died down a bit, we noticed the High Prince of Heaven heading off in quite the opposite direction. In fact He was making for the very wilderness which John had so recently left.

'What's happening?' we asked Michael. 'Wherever is He going?'

'The Mighty One told Him to go off into the wilds and prepare for a battle with Lucifer,' we were told.

This stunned us at first. We had heard no Messenger being instructed to communicate this to Him, and I think we were finding it hard to adjust to the fact that the High Prince of Heaven and the Mighty One did not need us angels as a means of contact. They shared the same Spirit, so they could talk to each other without words. To a lesser degree, Lighted Ones nowadays have the same privilege. The Spirit of the Mighty One lives in them – He is part of them, and they are part of Him. But I'm jumping too far forward in my story.

That desert was a bleak place, as Hagar, Moses and Elijah had already discovered – a terrible spot in which to fight Lucifer – just sand, rocks and emptiness in all directions. A sense of evil brooded over everything.

'Bodyguard, leave Him!' ordered the Archangel Michael.

'But surely,' we whispered to one another, 'He needs angels now, more than ever before?'

The Chief Guardian seemed to share our opinion, because instantly he was standing before the Mighty One's Great Throne.

'Sovereign Lord,' he began, after the necessary 'Holy, Holy, Holy', 'the High Prince of Heaven has forgotten to take any provisions with Him, so how are we to nourish Him? Can we pretend to be ravens as we did in the days of Elijah?'

'No,' said the Mighty One sadly, 'He will fast in preparation for the battle.'[31]

Notes

1. 2 Chron. 16:9.
2. Matt. 1:20–25.
3. Luke 2:1–7.
4. Luke 2:8–20.
5. Luke 1:30–31.
6. Luke 2:22–24.
7. Luke 2:36–38.
8. Luke 2:35, *The Message.*
9. Matt. 2:1–2.
10. John 11:47–48.
11. Exod. 23:20–22.
12. Matt. 2:13–18.
13. Eccl. 10:1.
14. Heb. 2:16.
15. Matt. 2:19–23.
16. Heb. 2:14; 4:15.
17. Matt. 26:53.
18. Job 33:19–25.
19. Luke 2:41–50.
20. Isa. 42:1–4.
21. Luke 2:51.
22. Luke 2:19.
23. Matt. 13:54–57; Mark 3:20; John 7:3–5.
24. Matt. 3:1–4.
25. Eph. 6:16.
26. Matt. 5:27–28.
27. Matt. 5:21–22.
28. Matt. 3:5–12.
29. Luke 7:18–19, 23.
30. Matt. 3:17, *The Message.*
31. Matt. 4:1–11.

Chapter 10

Battle with Lucifer

F ortunately for you, angels weren't created to fast – just to serve. Earthlings find it most unpleasant because they need food at roughly four-hourly intervals. But going without it does help them to 'disconnect' from their bodies so that their spirits can soar unhampered. An Earthling can get closer to Heaven when fasting than at any other time.

But 40 days was taking fasting to extreme limits, particularly as the High Prince of Heaven was already lean. Towards the end of the fast we could see that He was almost too weak to walk at all. His Guardians, who had all withdrawn to watch him from behind the rocky hills, told us they felt thoroughly worried.

'He's in no fit state for a showdown with Lucifer,' they reported to us, for we all sensed that our enemy was preparing to attack.

'Your Exalted Majesty,' bleated the High Prince's leading

Guardian as he presented himself yet again before the Throne. 'What if Lucifer turns up with a million of his best fighters? What are we to do then?'

'If he were to come with an army, then you have permission to fight back and protect the High Prince,' replied the Mighty One. 'But Satan knows you would win, so he won't bring anyone else with him – he's far too clever for that.'

'So how *will* he come?' we all asked each other in nervous whispers, as we peered down from the windows of Heaven. 'Look at our Prince down there in that heat and dust! He's so weak and ill now that He couldn't fight a dormouse.'

Then we saw him – Lucifer himself – closing in for the kill. He hardly ever comes to Earth in person, but whenever he does, he always chooses a new disguise. He was not wearing his snake costume this time; he looked fat, comfortable, kindly, almost motherly as he waddled up to the rock where the High Prince of Heaven was resting.

'You poor thing,' he purred gently. 'Just look at the mess you're in – more than half starved. Are you *sure* you were told to fast this long? Isn't it a bit silly, when you have the power to turn every stone in this desert into a loaf of hot, newly-baked bread? By the way, are you *really* sure you could do that – after all, you've never done anything miraculous yet, have you? Don't you think you ought to try your power out before you use it for others?'

The High Prince was silent, not even bothering to look at him. After a long pause, Lucifer tried again, still using the gentle approach.

'You really *ought* to eat something, you know. It won't be a fair fight if you have to take me on in this sort of state. Just turn one little stone into a loaf, give yourself strength and we'll let battle commence.'

Slowly the High Prince of Heaven turned His head and looked at His enemy for the first time, and then down at the stone that Lucifer was holding out on a podgy, fat hand. Don't forget that our Prince was fully human, and He was extremely hungry. It must have seemed such sensible advice. Because He was human He had the same gift of choice that all humans have. He could decide to be independent and meet his own needs, or he could decide to obey His orders. The time during which He sat looking at the little piece of desert rock was perhaps the most dangerous moment in the entire history of the universe.

Finally, He said slowly, 'My Father told me to fast, and He hasn't told me to stop yet. His Great Book says that true life is all about following His instructions, not satisfying human needs.'

The homely, cuddly figure disappeared instantly. The first round was ours. But he was back before the High Prince of Heaven had time to recover. This time he looked a bit over-dressed for the scene. He wore a black pinstripe suit with a neat tie and carried a briefcase containing a small computer, a cell-phone and a neatly rolled umbrella.

Suddenly they were standing together high above the Earth, and right outside time – looking down from an angel's viewpoint.

'See all that,' Lucifer began briskly. 'All those great cities, stock-markets, armies, palaces, companies – they all belong to me. The Mighty One gave me the entire world long before time began. I rule Planet Earth; but that's what you want to do, isn't it? You've come here to my kingdom to take it away from me. If you stay I'll have to kill you – you know that, don't you? And I'll kill you in the most painful way I can possibly devise. But it doesn't have to end like that. If you became 'my man' – knelt down and worshipped me – I'd give it all to you right now. Think of the riches you could have; the ease; the comfort; the power. Come on, be sensible. You're enough of a human to hate the thought of torture and death.'

'The first of my Father's Ten Rules of Happiness says we must worship Him, and only Him,' replied the High Prince simply. 'He knows what He's doing, even if it means that He allows you to kill me.'

The dapper little businessman disappeared as abruptly as 'Mother Earth' had done, and Jesus sank back against a scorching rock to rest.

'Can't we shower Him with a little cool water?' pleaded His Guardians. The Mighty One shook His head; the battle was not over yet.

This time Lucifer appeared 'on stage', in the ceremonial costume of a religious leader. Our only small satisfaction was to hope that he was extremely hot inside its heavy folds. This time the two of them seemed to be standing on the highest pinnacle of the Temple in Jerusalem.

'Look, my dear,' began Lucifer in an oily, clerical voice, 'I've misjudged you. You didn't come here to seize political power, but to win the spirits of men. I can see that. So you must show them, once and for all, that you are their Messiah. You must do something dramatic that will attract instant attention. Remember the words in the Great Book that you are so fond of quoting? "If you have made the Lord your dwelling ... God will command His Angels ... to guard you in all your ways; they will lift you up in their hands, so that you will not strike your foot against a stone."[1] It says that in the Book, doesn't it? Well, test the promise – jump – let the angels catch you. A few supernatural stunts like that, and all the religious-minded people in the entire world will flock after you. If what the Great Book says is true, prove it to me.'

'Get away!' said the High Prince of Heaven sternly. 'Faith doesn't need proof.'

With a shriek of pure rage, the extravagantly robed figure exploded and was gone; and a nod from the Mighty One despatched clouds of angels to the exhausted figure who was huddled, unconscious with exhaustion, under the desert sun.[2] They sponged him, administered sips of water, changed his filthy clothes and finally cooked him a meal fit for the King that he was. Then they sang and danced the night away for Him by the light of their fire, until He laughed with delight and all the joy of Heaven came flooding back into His tired, haggard face. Only twice were we allowed to comfort Him during those 33 years, but that made the occasions all the more special.

*

We angels *love* going to the weddings of Lighted Ones. The two Guardians who have cared for the bride and groom since babyhood stand behind the couple as they are officially joined in the presence of witnesses. They unite their wings to form a huge canopy above their heads, and if other Earthlings are praying, the Mighty One lets them pour the blessings of Heaven all over the couple. The two Guardians work in partnership after that, to keep the couple close together in love, and nothing upsets the Guardians more than when the two Earthlings fail to make each other happy.

Soon after the High Prince had returned home from His desert battle, He had to attend a family wedding in the nearby village of Cana. His mother Mary was in charge of the catering, and she was extremely worried. Both families were very poor and she was trying to manage on a ridiculously low budget.

'Family hold back,' she whispered to her sons and daughters as the feast began. The atmosphere was a little stiff and strained until suddenly the High Prince arrived, late. Instantly He was the centre of fun and laughter, and at once the party became a roaring success.

It exasperates us angels when we see the way in which Earth-artists portray our High Prince. They make Him look severe, withdrawn and downright depressed. If He'd *really* been like that, Earthlings would never have flocked after Him, hanging on His every word. Joy attracts, but disapproving gloom repels humans – and angels, for that matter. No, He was the kind of man who sat about in pubs, talking to ordinary people about ordinary things, cracking jokes, and telling stories which gripped people's imaginations and changed their lives. It was the joy of Heaven that they saw in Him, and joy drew them like pins to a magnet. By the time He was 30 His eyes and mouth were surrounded by laughter lines, and no one who looked into His face ever forgot His smile. His eyes, too, were so full of tenderness and compassion that I suppose no artist will ever be able to capture His expression accurately.

Suddenly we angels caught sight of Mary hurrying through the crowd of wedding guests towards her eldest son, trying hard to keep a relaxed smile on her face. Over the last 30 years she had learnt increasingly to rely on Jesus for help in every situation, great and small.

'My son,' she whispered urgently, 'we've completely run out of wine! The disgrace will ruin the day for the bride and groom.' She knew, as well as we did, that the One who had invented grapes in the first place could easily create wine, but He had never yet done anything beyond the range of human ability. But surely the time had come? Then we saw Him get up from the table and quietly whisper something to one of the servants. How relieved the two Guardian Angels of the wedding couple looked – and so did Mary – when, a few minutes later, the servants began to refill the 12 water pots which stood near the front door. Something was definitely going to happen.

'Take a pitcher of this water and pour it out for the Guest of Honour,' the High Prince told them when the job was done. Mary looked a bit tense then – the insult of offering that man a cup of water would never be forgiven – but out splashed rich, red wine, tasting better than anything the guests had sampled in their lives.

To us it seemed typical of our High Prince of Heaven that the first time He used His supernatural powers was to save two friends from embarrassment, by making wine for their special party. Surely that ought to convince Earthlings that He is not the miserable killjoy that many religious people make Him out to be?

*

But don't go thinking that our High Prince was nothing but a bundle of laughs. He was often stern and always totally unpredictable. Soon after that wedding He, and a group of his fishermen friends, headed down south towards the Temple in Jerusalem.[3] He did *not* receive the adulation of the Jewish hierarchy, as we angels had hoped, but instead He committed what, to some of us, looked rather like political suicide!

Battle with Lucifer

The religious leaders, in the hopes of making a bit for themselves, had allowed the only part of the Temple where foreigners could go to become a noisy market instead of the quiet place of peace and prayer that it was intended to be. People came looking for God, and sometimes travelled halfway round the world to do so, only to be met by the cries of stall-holders and the bleating and bellowing of frightened animals.

'How *dare* you turn my Father's house into a pad for villains!' the High Prince shouted furiously. Every angel who happened to be watching gaped in surprise. We had never seen Him this angry before; nor had He ever been violent, yet He seized some ropes, made a whip and began lashing out vigorously in all directions. Ignoring all protests, He kicked over tables piled high with 'dirty' money, ripped open bird-cages, and sent sheep and cattle hurtling in all directions.

What a glorious scene of confusion! We angels love a good drama like that! Most Lighted Ones have a problem about anger – they think it's always wrong. But heavenly anger – the kind that comes as a result of seeing *someone else* wronged – often gives Earthlings the energy and courage to stand up for the rights of others and to change bad situations.

Once the High Prince had made His point, He threw down the whip and walked over to a group of disabled people, huddling together among the stone arches, badly frightened by the uproar. He healed them all and sent them off as free and exuberant as the caged birds and the sacrificial animals – leaping and dancing for pure joy.

He would have been a great deal more popular if He had taken Lucifer's advice and allowed us to lower Him from the Temple roof. In fact His official entrance into the Temple could hardly have made a worse impression; and it was quite a relief to his Guardians to get Him back to the relative safety of the North country.

But, as it turned out, their job was no easier up there! The following Sabbath, the High Prince went into the synagogue in Nazareth, where he had worshipped every week right from his boyhood.[4] Picking up the scroll – part of the book that Isaiah had written so many years before – He began to read aloud. Isaiah wrote a lot about the Messiah, as the Scholarly Angel was always telling us. The High Prince of Heaven turned straight to the Messiah's job description,[5] a passage the Jews knew very well indeed. Then, looking up at all those faces He knew so well, He said simply, 'Today this prophecy has come true.'

In words that you young angels will understand that means, 'I'm the Messiah – I'm here at last. I've been sent to cheer up the poor, mend the broken-hearted, set captives free and change the misery of those who grieve into something beautiful and precious.'

'The worst has happened!' screamed the demons who were on duty in the synagogue, as they rushed back to Lucifer in blind panic. 'He's announced Himself – publicly!'

'Silence Him!' they were told. 'Pour fear, anger and jealousy into that synagogue – incite the Earthlings to murder.'

Lucifer's Lot are brilliant at crowd control – you have to give them credit for that. There were hundreds of them working in the building that day, thought-planting madly.

'This man's our carpenter – the son of our old friend Joseph! How can He suddenly say He's the Messiah?'

'He's gone mad since he went to hear that preacher, John.'

'He'll bring disgrace – and danger – to the whole district if we don't take action quickly.'

Those demons did such a brilliant job that in a few minutes they'd transformed a respectable country congregation
into a lynch mob, ready to murder a member of their community, while telling themselves they were doing the will of
God! Oh dear, those Earthlings are such a gullible lot! They
dragged the High Prince to the nearest hill, intending to
throw Him over the jagged north face of the rock. Of course,
their efforts were quite futile; no Earthling crowd, however
large, can murder someone who is surrounded by Angel
Guardians. The gripping, clawing fingers of those angry men
were gently prized open, invisible feet tripped them up and
the carpenter simply walked away, leaving them confused
and slightly unnerved by His sudden disappearance.

✻

Well, that day was the start of three years of extraordinary
events. The High Prince of Heaven never travelled more than
80 miles from his birthplace, never wrote a book or became a
politician, but what He said and did during those three years
changed everything down there on Earth. Over His head, in
the atmosphere surrounding the Earth, the fight between
light and darkness, good and evil, raged more fiercely than
ever before. Lucifer was terrified by this time, and he massed
his forces into Israel[6] until there were so many demons there
that we angels could hardly move for them. They nearly
managed to kill Him on several other occasions,[7] and
wheedled their way inside a remarkably large number of
people, causing them to oppose Him constantly.

This tactic didn't work too well because He always ordered
the demons to leave; and His obvious authority over the Powers of Darkness only increased His fame and popularity.[8]

Once, in an eerie graveyard[9] by the sea, His friends were petrified when a wild man came hurtling towards them, roaring vicious abuse. We could clearly see that he had at least 6,000 demons living inside him.[10] Don't look surprised – that's perfectly possible, and with so many Fallen Angels roaming around Israel, searching for human bodies and voices to use in their master's service, any Earthling whose spirit was receptive to evil soon found that they were being controlled by hordes of very nasty lodgers. This poor man's mob made him so dangerously violent that his family had often tried to restrain him by chaining his arms and legs to iron rings in the solid rock. The demons gave him such phenomenal strength that he always managed to break the iron fetters as easily as if they had been woollen threads, and all night long he ranged over the hills or ran along the seashore cutting his naked body with sharp stones and howling like a demented animal.

The fearsome figure lurched towards the High Prince's boat as it landed on the lonely beach. The fishermen who were with Jesus were terrified. It was still well before dawn, but even in the grey half-light they could see that the beach was used as a burial place, and the dead bodies of Earthlings were left to rot in the caves which tunnelled into the cliff-side.

'It's a ghost!' they screamed, as they fell over each other in their hurry to climb back on board; but the High Prince quietly walked towards the frightful creature, with nothing but concern in His eyes for the mess that Lucifer had made of him.

'What do you want with us?' screamed the demons, using the man's voice. 'We know who you are, Son of the Most High God! Don't torture us!'

'What is your name?' the High Prince asked the man steadily.

'Legion,' came the reply, 'because there are so many of us.' Then the voice changed into a whine as the demons began to plead for their freedom. 'Don't send us to the Abyss – please don't!'[11] That's exactly where they deserved to go, but, for some reason that we angels could not understand, the High Prince allowed them to enter a herd of pigs, feeding in the fields above the beach. The terrified animals stampeded towards the cliff edge, and wave after wave of them hurtled over the top and disappeared into the sea, squealing madly. The watching farm-hands peered after them in open-mouthed astonishment, and then turned and sprinted away in the opposite direction.

Legion, the man who had looked so ferocious and wild a minute before, suddenly seemed small, fragile and embarrassed about his lack of clothing. Gently, the High Prince covered him with his own cloak, shared His packet of food, then helped him to wash. Finally, He found him a spare set of clothes in the boat and by the time a huge crowd of indignant villagers arrived on the scene Legion was looking completely normal and remarkably happy.

The whole neighbourhood was so stunned by the sight of him (and the loss of their pigs) that they begged Jesus to go away.

'Let me come with you,' pleaded Legion. Jesus shook His head gently.

'I need you to go and tell all the people in the district just how kind God has been to you,' He said. 'I'll come back again soon, when you've prepared their hearts for me.' And that is exactly what Legion did. In fact, he told his story so well that when the High Prince returned, crowds of enthusiastic listeners were eagerly waiting for Him.[12]

Lucifer was far too clever to go on using a military tactic which was clearly not being successful, so he rapidly changed his plans and tried a much more subtle approach. He realized that the religious 'do-gooders' made better allies than more openly occult extremists. The proud Pharisees were so busy trying to keep all of God's Ten Rules, and hundreds more that they had made up themselves, that they completely forgot to love.[13] Lucifer managed to gain control of their minds, because they so badly wanted to be admired by the people, and the carpenter's popularity was fast eclipsing their own reputations.

Yes? You over there, you've got a question? Why didn't the Jewish leaders recognize the Messiah they'd been waiting for, for so long? Because He wasn't the kind of Messiah they expected. They thought He'd be much more aloof, noble and distant – like John, who baptized in the Jordan. They were sure that the *real* Messiah wouldn't sit about in pubs talking to prostitutes and taxmen; wouldn't waste His time helping the homeless or crippled children – He would get on and *do* something about the Romans. Their stereotyped Messiah wouldn't have told stories about forgiveness and wouldn't have urged people to love and pray for their enemies, and never to fight back.[14] They wanted a swashbuckling superman.

His huge popularity was their biggest problem, and He was such a lovable person that they couldn't fault Him – until He played into their hands[15] and began to drop an increasing number of hints about His real identity. For instance, He told them that He'd been alive before Abraham,[16] and that He could forgive sins.[17]

'Blasphemy!' they yelled. 'He's making himself out to be God now! That settles the matter – He must be either completely mad or a wicked impostor. We're going to have to shut Him up before He causes everyone one of us permanent damage.'

It causes me even more pain to have to tell you that the High Prince's own family were also influenced by demonic thought-planting. Like I said, His brothers had always been a bit jealous of the way Mary adored her first-born, but they tolerated Him while He ran the family business so successfully. Once He left home, though, and began 'roaming round the country on a massive ego trip' (their description), they began to get angry.

'He's gone right over the top!' they told each other. 'Megalomania – people like that often think they're the Messiah when really they're stark raving mad. We'll just have to go and bring him home by force before he disgraces the entire family.'[18] But, like everyone else, they were entirely powerless against our High Prince.

In spite of all the horrible things that the Others were doing to Him, He just went on loving people and using His supernatural powers to help them.

He knew that humans would find it easier to understand how much they were loved by God if they could see love demonstrated in the actions of a human like themselves. So He showed them what it means to love by the way He cared about the hungry, the disabled, little children and people who felt they were 'no hopers'. How proud we angels were of Him!

We never left His side, but He needed human friends too. Wherever He went He was always surrounded by a group of people who gave up all they had to travel with Him from village to village.[19]

'He's teaching them so that, in time, they can go off and show others how to love,' explained Gabriel, but the rest of us couldn't help wondering why Our Prince chose people like them for such an important job. They weren't particularly intelligent, and their lights often burned alarmingly low. Their leader was a huge fisherman called Simon Peter, a tactless loudmouth of the very worst kind; but in spite of his hilarious blunders he really loved our High Prince – which, like I said, is all that matters.

My, those disciples got tired at first![20] The lifestyle was exhausting – the surging crowds, endless travelling and the constant, exhausting demands of suffering people – but oh, they did have fun together! All the Guardians on duty with them said it was much more like Heaven than Earth. I think it's the laughter that Lighted Ones notice most when they first arrive up here in Heaven. They aren't surprised by the music – they expect that – but they never expect angels to laugh, yet we do it all the time.

After a while the High Prince began to allow His followers to share His power. He showed them how to heal the sick and even gave them authority over enemy agents. 'Now, off you go,' He told them one day. 'Practise what I've been teaching you. Go and tell people the good news that I've come to set their spirits alight.'

We had to laugh! Those men made so many mistakes at first, and they were so scared! Then gradually they found that they could do the same things that He could do – and they were thrilled when blind eyes opened and crippled legs straightened under their hands!

'It works!' they told Him ecstatically when they eventually found Him again. 'And even the demons do as we tell them – just like they do for you!'

Now, it's important that you lot know this. *All* Lighted Ones have the power to help others by doing the same supernatural things that the High Prince did. He even told them they could do greater things,[21] but, sadly, only a handful of them have ever taken Him at His word and actually used His power.

*

We think He found it quite hard living with those friends of His because they, like most Earthlings, found it so hard to believe. There was one particular night when they were all out in a fishing boat and a totally unexpected severe storm hit them. Water terrifies Earthlings, perhaps because they can't control it, particularly when it's whipped into huge waves by an angry wind. Some of those disciples were positively climbing the masts with pure terror as the storm howled around them. Just try to think how you would feel if you had no wings! Angels can rise safely out of any nasty Earth situation and be somewhere else in the universe in less than a second. So it is hard for you to realize how totally stuck in their own limited environment your new charges are going to be. And always keep reminding yourselves that they can't see you there beside them, when they're in danger.

While those 12 men were panicking, screaming with fear, eyes rolling and teeth chattering, all Heaven was laughing at them – in a kindly way, of course. You see, that boat was surrounded by more than 12,000 angels – the entire bodyguard of the High Prince – and each of those men had a large group of personal Guards because they were Vitally Important People in their own right.

We were all round the boat, laughing with pure joy as we rode the great waves like Earthling surfers. There were so many angels in the water under the boat that she was almost riding on our shoulders. There were angels flying among the storm-clouds overhead and whirling and swirling with delight in the wind. There were even angels *in* the boat, pushing their fingers in the holes as they appeared in the hull, or holding the mast safely in position. That boat could not possibly have sunk, because the 'time had not come' for any of them. Lighted Ones never need to fear danger – we're always there to protect them; and, even if they have reached the end of their appointed time on Earth, they have no cause to fear death because, as I've told you before, it's our job to take them to the place where their real life begins. Yes, if only they *believed* that, how peaceful their lives could be.

It was no wonder that the High Prince was cross with His friends when they rudely woke Him up from a deep sleep by shouting, 'Don't you care that we're all about to die?'[22] He promptly silenced the storm as effortlessly as an Earthling blows out a match, but we could see that He was disappointed. 'Why ever were you so scared?' He asked them. 'Have you *still* no faith in Me?'

You'll soon realize just how exasperating humans can be – their trust grows so slowly. But then, I suppose they can't see into the real world – they just have to decide to believe in it. Perhaps faith pleases the Mighty One so enormously simply because it's so rare.

Do you remember me telling you that children always seem to be far more susceptible to us and the heavenly dimension than adult Earthlings? Well, we angels think they're also far more discerning – they know instinctively when they are wanted by other Earthlings, or when they are secretly disapproved of and rejected. We think that is probably why the High Prince seemed to draw children wherever He went. Even when he was talking serious stuff to self-important men, some child would always manage to wriggle into the centre of the group, to lean up against His knee or squat at His feet. They knew they were safe with Him, you see. Whenever He walked into a village, hot and dusty from His journey, every Child-Guardian in the place would hurry their small charges in His direction for His blessing, and, in no time, He'd have a thick cluster of children and their angels all round him. They would all sit for hours, wide-eyed, listening to His stories. Nothing ever delighted Him, or those Guardians, more than when He healed the crippled limbs of a child, sending them skipping and hopping away with their friends. Sometimes the High Prince's disciples thought that He wasted too much time and precious energy on these children, who were considered very unimportant in those days.[23] That always upset Him badly, and He'd tell those grown men that they needed to become as innocent and trusting as children if they wanted to be part of His Kingdom.[24]

Watching the High Prince lovingly care for children, nothing could have prepared us for the next part of the story.

Notes

1. Ps. 91:9–12.
2. Matt. 4:11.
3. John 2:13–21.
4. Luke 4:14–30.
5. Isa. 61:1–3.

6. Dr Arnold G. Fruchtenbaum, *Satanology: the Doctrine of Satan* (Ariel Ministries Press, PO Box 3723, Tustin, CA 92681, USA).

7. Matt. 8:24–25; John 8:59.

8. Luke 4:33–35.

9. Mark 5.

10. Luke 8:30. A Roman legion consisted of approximately 6,000 soldiers.

11. 2 Pet. 2:4.

12. Luke 8:38–40.

13. Luke 18:10–12.

14. Matt. 5:43–45.

15. John 8:46.

16. John 8:48.

17. Luke 5:21.

18. Mark 3:20–21.

19. Luke 6:12–13; 8:1–3; 10:23, 44.

20. Mark 3:20.

21. John 14:12.

22. Luke 8:22–25.

23. Matt. 19:13–15.

24. Matt. 18:3.

Chapter 11

Angels in Anguish

After the High Prince had been showing His love to mankind for about three years, we angels began to realize that Lucifer was getting his forces ready for a major military offensive. Michael despatched extra Warrior Angels to reinforce the Guardians, but Lucifer is clever. He was still doing all his dirty work through religious men,[1] who surrounded the High Prince like a venomous cloud of wasps as the situation gradually worsened.[2]

It never occurred to us that the great Warrior Angels could fail to protect the High Prince of Heaven, or that any harm could ever come to Him. Even though our Prince told His friends, on several occasions, that His enemies would manage to kill him eventually, somehow our angel minds could never take it in – the thought was just too horrific. All the same, as the fateful Passover Festival drew near, with its great annual trek to the Temple, we became very uneasy.

'If only the High Prince would just stay away from Jerusalem,' we told each other, 'protecting Him would be so much easier for us.' But He would never dodge danger, unless He had specific orders. So, as usual, He and His friends set out for the capital, just as they always did at Passover time.

As they walked up the long road which led to Jerusalem, we could all see that the High Prince was aware of His danger. Instead of walking with His friends, laughing, joking and telling them stories, He trudged along by Himself, ahead of the group – His face set, hard as a flint-stone wall. The only time it relaxed into a smile was when he was delayed by a leper who wanted to say 'thank you',[3] a blind beggar[4] and a lonely little taxman who'd shinned up a tree to catch a glimpse of Him.[5] He always had time for people like that, however much He had on his mind.

When He finally reached the hill overlooking the great city of Jerusalem He stopped, and for a long time He was silent. His friends, taking the chance to rest, sprawled in the silvery shade of the olives. They didn't speak: there was something about His expression that silenced even Peter. We were restless, too, as we looked down from millions of vantage points in the clouds. He was deeply distressed, we could see that, but what was He thinking? His Guardians pressed in closely around Him, while their leader asked the Mighty One how they could comfort Him.

'There is no comfort for love that is not returned,' whispered the Mighty One in a broken voice. 'Look, my Son is weeping. The gift of choice that we gave mankind is infinitely costly.'

And He *was* weeping – sobbing, in fact – as He stood there under the gnarled trunks of the olive trees.

'Oh Jerusalem, Jerusalem,' we heard Him say, 'I sent My Prophets to tell you how much I love you, and longed to protect you and care for you, but you wouldn't have My love. You stoned My messengers to death and broke My Rules of Happiness; and all I wanted was to comfort you, as a hen gathers her chicks safe under her wings.'[6]

He might have been seeing Jerusalem as it was going to be in just a few years' time – nothing but a heap of rubble covering the corpses of thousands of its murdered inhabitants. But we angels think He was weeping for the whole of humanity as well at that moment, and all Heaven grieved for Him and with Him.

'Surely this is only a temporary situation,' one of us whispered to Gabriel. 'They couldn't reject His love for much longer, surely? Not when He's gone down there to live with them.'

The voice of the irritating Scholarly Angel did nothing to lift our spirits. 'They *do* reject him,' he said. 'Look, it's all written up in the Book of Isaiah.'[7] We pretended that we hadn't heard him, but angels weren't created to be rude – just to serve.

The next few days were most uncomfortable. We watched Lucifer wooing Judas Iscariot and gradually penetrating his spirit. We watched enemy agents planting murderous thoughts in the minds of Pharisees, priests and members of parliament, and we saw the High Prince's friends totally failing to see the danger that was engulfing them, because they were too busy quarrelling over their future government positions when He came into power. How little they understood!

Then on Passover Eve, the High Prince asked His 12 close friends to share the traditional family meal with Him, in a little attic room high above the narrow back streets of

Jerusalem.[8] It was not the happy occasion that Passover Feasts usually were. A sense of doom hung over the group and, as we angels stood behind our charges, we could see the tension on their faces magnified and distorted by the flickering lamp-light. Earlier that day we had seen Judas selling our High Prince for a few grubby bits of silver.[9] He was planning to meet the Temple guards later that evening so that he could lead them to the garden outside the city wall where the High Prince often loved to camp out for the night under the stars.

'Judas won't be allowed to do this,' we told each other. 'Remember Baalam and his talking donkey? One of the Warriors was allowed to stop his evil errand. Perhaps we'll be told to block the street and stop Judas getting to his rendezvous with the Temple guards. Or we could even strike the whole rabble blind before they reach the garden – we've done that before now! Or we could terrify them with unearthly sounds if they *do* arrive there.'

When Judas finally left the table and went off into the dark, shadowy streets, we were totally confident that we would be given our orders for dealing with him – or anyone else, for that matter.

The High Prince had so many things on His heart that night, and He obviously longed to share them with these Earthlings whom He loved so much. He warned them that trouble was on its way and, looking back, we angels can understand why He looked so sad as He told them that, for not one of those eager young men who smiled back at Him in the lamp-light was going to avoid acute suffering. They would be stoned, publicly beaten, shipwrecked, accused, tried unfairly, tortured, executed – and Peter the fisherman would even be crucified upside down by the Romans. The High Prince knew all that as He looked into their eyes.

'But don't let yourself get worried and upset about anything,' He told them gently. 'I'm going on ahead of you to get everything ready in My Father's House; but I'll come back and take you there some day, and then we can always be together.' He was trying so hard to describe Heaven and eternity in words that they would understand, but we could see that they were as confused as Earthlings always are when they try to picture our world. How can you explain the unexplainable to beings with such limited brains?

'You'll all have your own houses up there in my Father's Home – lovely mansions. And I'll be there with you, and nothing will ever separate us – ever again.'

'But we don't understand you!' shouted Thomas, bringing his fist down on the table with a heart-rending degree of desperation. 'We don't know what you're talking about. Where are you going and how will we ever find the way there?'

'I am the way, Thomas,' replied the High Prince gently. 'No one reaches the Father without Me. I am the bridge which links Earth and Heaven.'

We could see that the poor things couldn't take it in, and yet it was so pathetically obvious to us angels.

'And now,' continued the High Prince, 'I want to give you all something that has been very precious to Me. I'll bequeath it to you as your inheritance. I don't have money, possessions or even property to leave you, but I have My peace[10] and My joy.[11] Whatever you have to face in the future, if you have inner peace and joy, you'll cope with it. Live constantly in Me and My love.[12] Anything you do without Me is totally useless. And love one another in the same way I *love* you – that's an order.'

There hasn't been a Lighted Earthling since that moment who has ever consistently obeyed that command, and yet it was the very heart of all that He had come to Earth to tell them!

Then He prayed for them, His beautiful, loving words echoing to the furthest crannies of Heaven. I'll never forget how He finished.

'Righteous Father, the world has never known You, but I have known You, and these disciples know You because You sent Me on this mission. I have made Your very being known to them – who You are and what You do – and I continue to make it known so that Your love for Me might be in them. As they love one another with that love, the rest of the world will believe that You sent Me.'[13]

After that, they were off into the back alleyways which led to the city gate.

'Could we encourage Him *not* to stop in Gethsemane tonight?' the leading Guardian asked the Mighty One. 'It would be far safer if He went to stay with His friends out at Bethany.' But the Mighty One was silent; He did not even appear to hear our entreaties. We angels were getting worried (even though angels were not created to worry, just to serve). That was a very bad night for us. Even the Watcher Angels surrounding Judas Iscariot reported that his mission was being totally successful.

When the little group of 12 men reached the garden called Gethsemane, most of them wrapped themselves in their cloaks and were asleep on the grass in a few moments.[14]

'I need you,' we heard the High Prince say to the three men closest to Him. 'Please don't go to sleep. Sit up and keep Me company.'

'You can count on us, Master!' said Peter, and promptly fell fast asleep – and the other two soon joined him. Turning sadly away, the High Prince walked alone into the olive grove. Terrible anxiety and foreboding was obviously pressing Him down. As we watched, we saw Him fall to the ground, crying out to the Mighty One in an agony of fear.

'Father, don't let this happen to Me! Surely there has to be some other way ...' His words were echoed by every angel in Heaven, as we had to watch Him writhing there in the shadows. Lucifer's chief agents were posted all round Him, skulking behind the twisted trunks of the olive trees.

'Take this cup away from me, Father,' the High Prince pleaded again, His face distorted, bathed in blood and sweat.[15]

There was no answer from Heaven – I don't suppose He expected one.

'It's not what I want that matters, Father, but what You want,' He whispered finally. Then, chilled by the silence, He went to find His human friends. They were still sleeping soundly.

As He turned away He must have felt totally abandoned. Once again human beings had let Him down. How we ached for Him. Then, at last the order we'd all been longing for came, crisp and brief.

'Comfort Him.'[16] The Guardians closed in around Him, their wings a wall of invisible protection against the sneering demons in the trees. Their voices sounded like doves cooing on a warm summer evening as they poured the strength of Heaven into his tired body, and the rest of us sighed with relief because we knew that no Earthling army could ever penetrate their defences. Obviously the last hour had only been a test of obedience, as when Abraham had been ordered to sacrifice his son; and then, at the last possible moment, our Prince would be let off, just as Abraham had been before him.[17]

Then, suddenly, we heard the sound of stealthy footsteps approaching down the path from Jerusalem, and we saw the glint of knives in the starlight.[18] They were coming for Him. There was no time to be lost! We knew those Guardians had to get him out *now*! Heaven waited tensely for the order to evacuate, but when the sound of the Mighty One's voice finally boomed out across the universe, we shrank back in horror. The terrible command sounded like cannon-fire, magnified a billion times as it echoed round the galaxies:

'Angels! Stand back!' I never heard His voice sound so harsh; and the sound of it sent an icy draught all over Heaven. 'Stand back, I say!'

For millions of years we angels had been receiving all kinds of orders from the Mighty One, but never was there one which strained our obedience more than that one. Yes, standing back and leaving the High Prince of Heaven at that moment was definitely the hardest thing we angels ever had to do.

For a fraction of a second not one of those Guardians moved – they remained with their wings enclosing Him protectively. They had been there with him right from the moment of His conception. How could they stand back now? But the High Prince heard the order and He also heard the footsteps.

'Go,' He told them firmly as He rose to face His friend Judas and his traitor's kiss.

And there stood our Prince, totally alone, facing a group of thugs and bullies who were out for His blood. Most of His human attendants ran off into the shadows with quite amazing speed, and His heavenly attendants were bound by cords of obedience. The only person left to defend him was that oaf of a fisherman swinging a rusty old sword he had never used before in his life.

'Put it away, Peter,' the High Prince said – sounding almost amused. 'Don't you know that I could have 72,000 angels here right now, battle ready and armed to the teeth – if I asked for them?' We cheered up at the very thought, knowing that the Mighty One would certainly change our orders if the High Prince asked Him to. Peter obviously preferred to put his trust in feeble human strength, and off came the nearest bully's ear.

Even at a moment like that, the High Prince couldn't resist staunching the blood with the hem of his own cloak, replacing the ear and then healing the wretched man's wound completely.

*

I'm sorry, class, but you'll have to be patient with me. You must understand that the events of the next few hours were terrible for us angels to watch – in fact they were the most difficult in the entire span of Earth-time for every one of us in Heaven. We had to stand there, immobilized and totally powerless, while the men our Prince had created for love turned on Him in pure hatred. They kicked him, punched his head, lied disgustingly, accused him unfairly and yelled endless volleys of abuse. All He ever wanted to do was show them how to live forever, but they unleashed on His undefended head all the fury of hell. When those Roman whips began to cut deep into his back, we angels were in indescribable anguish. In fact the terrible order 'Stand back!' had to be repeated on several occasions – otherwise many of us might have forgotten ourselves completely. How could they be allowed to treat their Creator like that? Mute, and almost mutinous, we watched as His bruised and bleeding body was

dragged through the dust of Jerusalem and humiliated in
every possible way.[19] But He still didn't call for help.

Of course, Lucifer loved it. 'I warned him I'd kill Him one
day,' he cackled. 'He should have bowed down and worshipped me while He had the chance. This'll teach Him to
challenge my right to rule Planet Earth.'

They put a rough wooden cross on His raw, bleeding back.
It was too heavy for Him to carry, and we longed to lift it for
Him, but another terrible 'Stand back!' held us in check.

Through the streets they drove Him, whipping Him mer-
cilessly every time He stumbled. Earthlings looked on
impassive – uncaring, yet those people *knew* Him. Some He'd
healed, others He'd fed, and many had been given back their
hope and self-respect by just one look from His eyes. How
can Earthlings change so suddenly? A few women whose
spirits were alight wept as He stumbled by, but most people
simply looked the other way.[20] Why didn't they all rise up
and defend Him? How could they let their Messiah die like
an animal?

At the top of a bleak hill they nailed Him to the cross and
swung Him high, facing the city He loved so much.[21]

'Oh Jerusalem, Jerusalem, how often I would have gathered you, but you would not …' His words were still fresh in
our memories – this just *couldn't* be happening! Good *had* to
triumph over evil! Lucifer *couldn't* be allowed to kill a part of
God himself! How we longed to pull out those cruel nails and
lift Him far away from that dreadful, ungrateful planet, but
instead of asking for our help He pleaded with the Mighty
One to forgive them.[22]

Twelve legions of the mightiest Warriors in Heaven stood
at attention, with their swords drawn – enough to wipe out
the entire universe in less than a moment. He didn't have to

hang there – He had the gift of choice – but He stayed where He was, right to the very end.

We were in such acute distress that for a long time we did not dare to look at the Mighty One Himself, fearing that the sight of His suffering would be totally beyond our endurance. Then, when I finally dared to peep, I was horrified to see that He was standing, glaring down at His Son – a look of terrible, vengeful anger on His face.

'He blames the High Prince for every sin that has ever been committed,' Gabriel whispered, seeing my confusion. 'He is pouring out the terrible righteous wrath of Heaven over Him. I wouldn't look if I were you – it's too awful a sight, even for an angel.'

Gabriel was right, and I covered my eyes, too full of grief to speak. He was being punished for all the selfish, mean things that those Earthlings had done to one another, and I still could not understand why. Thick, suffocating darkness covered the Earth,[23] and even the lights of Heaven were dim. In the terrible silence we could hear Lucifer's mocking laughter. He thought this was his final triumph.

Then a terrible cry cut the air: 'My God, why have you forsaken me?'

We angels knew that this suffering would be far worse for our Prince than the physical agony. To feel the weight of His Father's terrible displeasure, and to be separated from His love by the great wall of His furious anger – that would be frightful indeed. Yet still He did not call for our help. Then suddenly, as His human heart finally broke, He gasped, 'It's finished.'

'He's at the point of death,' said Gabriel. 'Get ready to bring Him up here safely. Prepare the chariots of fire, lay out the welcome feast, and launch the festivities.' Eagerly we sprang into action, but again the same terrible order rang through Heaven:

'Stand back! Sinners do not come up here to Heaven when they die.' We froze, stunned by this fresh horror – the worst one of all.

We heard the High Prince gasp out His last words: 'Father, I place into Your hands My spirit.' But instead of carrying His spirit on a million wings safely back to His Father's home, we had to watch Lucifer's agents drag it roughly down to hell, tearing at it with their horrible fangs and claws.

You ought to know that when Earthlings refuse to ask forgiveness for their sins, and deliberately choose to turn away from the Mighty One's love, then that is what happens to their spirits when their bodies die.[24] Hell is such a terrible place that we angels try never to think about it. But the Mighty One spared his Son *nothing*, not even hell.[25] We could no longer see Him, but we were aware that a terrible fight raged over the High Prince during the next three days.

His Earthling family and friends knew nothing of all that, naturally, but how they wept as they buried His lacerated, blood-stained body in a cave not far from where He died.[26]

His earthly enemies did not realize the battle that was still raging either, as they smugly patted themselves on the back and went home to wash their hands of the troublemaker from the North country.

The Romans posted guards outside the cave, 'just in case', and Heaven waited numb and silent with grief. And all the while the battle went on in hell. The power and energy of every demon was concentrated on keeping the High Prince a prisoner there, but His power was far too great for theirs. When He had tasted the bitter consequences of sin to the fullest possible extent, and been tortured to the extreme limits of the lowest parts of hell, He burst out of the darkness, scattering evil spirits in all directions and, with a shout of triumph, He and millions of others were free from death and hell for ever.

An earthquake rattled the rocky graveyard at dawn, and one of the top angels was sent to roll back the huge stone that blocked the mouth of the cave in the limestone rockface.[27] It was so huge that it had taken six men to push it into place, but with one finger the great angel flipped it aside and sat on it. The squad of soldiers standing guard were stiff with fear. To them He looked like lightning and his clothes were dazzlingly white, like fresh snow. One after another, they sank senseless to the ground, like trees felled by a storm. For a long time they lay there rigid, unable to move for sheer terror. Then, as all the choirs in Heaven sang with joy, the blazing Spirit of the High Prince of Heaven entered the mangled, lifeless body which was laid out neatly on the stone slab in the darkness. It rose instantly, right through the bandages that bound it like a mummy. Angel attendants dressed Him in a new set of clothes, and the High Prince of Heaven stepped out into the early morning sunshine and smiled at the rows of angels lined up in military formation to welcome Him.

Then we *knew*! Lucifer had *not* won; in fact he had been finally defeated.[28] The High Prince of Heaven Himself had been punished in the place of every single sinful Earthling who had chosen to turn away from the Mighty One. He had taken away the sin that walled them off from God and made friendship with Him impossible. No longer would they have to use an animal as a sacrifice; this most perfect of all human beings had become a sacrifice for all time.[29]

'He *knew* it was going to be like this,' muttered Gabriel, 'but why didn't we realize it before? He must have known He'd have to die to achieve what He wanted most – friendship with the Earthlings He loves so much.'

Suddenly the same realization came to us all. The High Prince's words flooded back to us. He had said He was going to die and rise again so many times – how could we not have understood?[30]

Even the voice of the Scholar Angel did not irritate us that day. 'It was all foretold 700 years ago by Isaiah,' he said, piously fumbling through the great scrolls. 'Yes, here it is … here's what Isaiah wrote:[31] "We despised Him and rejected Him, He endured suffering and pain... But He endured the suffering that should have been ours; the pain that we should have borne. Because of our sins He was wounded; beaten because of the evil we did. We are healed by the punishment He suffered, made whole by the blows he received." It's all here. The High Prince of Heaven and the Mighty One must have planned it all before time even began.'

Then all the orchestras and brass bands of Heaven joined the massed choirs, and the noise must have deafened the demons as they sulked at the bottom of hell. They were beaten! And they were beginning to realize it.

While we were all still enjoying ourselves, singing and dancing for joy all over the graveyard, the soldiers slowly began to come round and, rubbing their eyes, they watched us for a while.[32] Then, very shakily, they got up and ran like startled rabbits. Deserting their posts was a crime punishable by death, but they preferred to face an angry centurion rather than Heaven's Warriors!

Later a group of women came down the path towards us. Their shoulders drooped with sadness, their poor faces were haggard with grief and lack of sleep.[33]

'Comfort them,' came the order, and two Messengers were actually permitted to appear in their brightest and most shining costumes. Far from being comforted, the poor women were terrified – at first.

'Don't be alarmed,' the Messengers told them hastily – remembering the fainting soldiers. 'We know you're looking for Jesus of Nazareth, but He's not here – He's risen from the dead. Look, here's the slab of stone where His body was lying. So why are you looking among the dead for someone who is alive?' Then they added gently, 'Remember, He told you it would all happen like this.'

'Of course!' gasped the women, as the words of the High Prince came flooding back to their minds too. They were so ecstatic that they forgot to be afraid.

'Go and tell His friends what's happened,' said the Angels, and then they disappeared.

The women ran almost as fast as the soldiers had done, but there was joy in their hearts, not terror. 'We've seen angels!' they gasped, bursting into the attic room, which had become the group's headquarters. 'They told us that the Lord is alive and has gone to Galilee.'

'Angels?' said the men. 'You say you saw angels? Grief is playing tricks on you. Angels indeed! That's women's nonsense!'

We were so upset! Calling angels nonsense, and at a time like that too! Those poor women went straight back to the garden, doubting their own sanity. But over the next 40 days the High Prince of Heaven appeared personally to all His friends, either individually or in small groups or in large gatherings,[34] and finally banished all doubt from their minds.

He was still wearing his human body, with its many terrible wounds, and He shared many meals with His friends.

They saw him eat fish and bread, but He was also able to walk through walls and become invisible at will, just as we angels can.[35] Strange! Yet another mystery that we angels feel is quite beyond us.[36]

Then one morning He took His friends to the hill outside Jerusalem where He had once stood and wept with disappointed love.[37]

'Go *everywhere* and tell *everyone* about me,' He told them. 'Don't just stay here in Israel – go all over the Earth. Tell every human being how they can live for ever, and how they can become my friends because I died for them on that cross. Set their spirits on fire with love for God and other people too. Go, and I'll always be with you, until the very end of time. Wait in Jerusalem until I come to you by My Spirit. It is *through* my Spirit that I will give you all the power you need.'

Then, right in front of them, He began to float upwards into the golden glory of sunset clouds.[38] He did not leave His body behind on Earth as other men do, but it rose, effortlessly, until we had covered him from their view with our outstretched wings.

The 11 men were left standing, opened mouthed, gazing at an empty sky.

'Comfort them,' came the order, and we were glad of that. We could guess how forlorn they would feel when the shock had worn off a bit. Two Messengers appeared beside them in plain white clothes, with subdued lighting – they didn't want to frighten the apostles too much.

'You Galileans!' They had to speak quite sharply to get their attention. 'Why are you standing here, gazing at the sky? Jesus has gone back to Heaven, but you can be certain that He'll come back, just as you saw Him go.'

For many days those Earthlings existed in a kind of vacuum, huddled fearfully in their attic hideout.[39] They knew something was about to happen but they were not quite sure what. I have to admit, we angels were in the same awkward position; the Mighty One and the High Prince didn't take us into their confidence.[40]

Then early one morning something happened which we angels still can't fathom.[41] The Spirit of the Mighty One and the High Prince descended like a great fireball, and hovered over the heads of all those Lighted Ones as they prayed in their attic. Flames of fire rested on each of them, and gradually penetrated their spirits, increasing their brightness a hundred times over. It was such a beautiful sight that we longed to be able to cry tears of joy. In the past the Spirit of the Mighty One had often been *with* Earthlings, but suddenly the Living God Himself was *in* them, filling them, possessing them, permeating their minds and emotions and taking control of their entire beings. Wonderful![42] The Great Creator of the Universe, who is so vast that Heaven itself is not big enough to contain Him, was making His home inside those little human bodies.

And do you know what happened then? All those Lighted Ones suddenly began to talk in our angelic language – all at once at the tops of their voices! We were so thrilled that *we* were speechless![43]

Notes

1. Matt. 21:33–39.
2. Ps. 22:12–13.
3. Luke 17:12–19.
4. Luke 18:35–43.

5. Luke 19:1–9.
6. Luke 13:34–35.
7. Isa. 53:3.
8. Mark 14:12–17.
9. Luke 22:3–6.
10. John 14:27.
11. John 15:11.
12. John 15:1–8.
13. John 17:21–26.
14. Matt. 26:36–46.
15. Isa. 54:14.
16. Luke 22:43.
17. Gen. 22:1–19.
18. Matt. 26:47.
19. Isa. 53:5–7.
20. Luke 23:27.
21. Luke 23:33.
22. Luke 23:34.
23. Matt. 27:45.
24. Matt. 13:49–50; 2 Thess. 1:7–9.
25. 1 Pet. 3:18; Eph. 4:8–9.
26. Matt. 27:57–61.
27. Matt. 28:1–4.
28. Col. 2:15.
29. Heb. 7:26–27.
30. Mark 9:31–32.
31. Isa. 54.
32. Matt. 28:11.
33. Luke 24:1–12.
34. 2 Cor. 15:3–6.
35. Luke 24:36–42; John 20:26–28.
36. 1 Pet. 1:12.

37. Matt. 28:16–20.
38. Acts 1:9–11.
39. Acts 1:12–14.
40. Acts 1:7.
41. Acts 2:1–4.
42. John 14:19–20, 23.
43. Acts 2:4; 1 Cor. 13:1.

Chapter 12

The Big Change

A fter the fire of Heaven descended on the attic room a huge change came about in the universe. The Mighty One no longer looks down on the Earth, controlling things from a vast distance – He actually lives there Himself these days. Of course, such a thing could never have happened without that horrible affair of the cross. That's what made it possible for Him to come close to Earthlings. In fact, He couldn't possibly get closer – He's part of the very cells of their bodies. Amazing! As they walk about the Earth, they not only have Him living in *them*, but they also live in *Him*. They move and have their complete existence encased in the Mighty One Himself.[1] He is so close that He is part of them and they are part of Him. This is totally different from the way He is with us. Angels weren't created to be His body, just to serve.

Yes, all that was definitely a huge change, but the Mighty One loves change. New ways of doing things – new ideas, new plans; all that is the breath of life to Him. He's creative, you see – the Father of all innovators.[2]

After the Big Change, Lighted Ones had all the authority of Heaven at their disposal, and they could communicate with the Mighty One so much more easily. We were all astounded at the difference which that fact made to those first Earthling Christians. No sooner had the fireball exploded over them than they were all rushing out into the street – fear of the Jews gone completely – and all their shyness. They told everyone who would listen all about the High Prince of Heaven. By the end of the day, Jerusalem was illuminated by 3,000 new Lights. Wonderful!

During the next years these Lights exploded in all directions, right over the civilized world.[3] The High Prince's followers took the wonderful news over seas, deserts, mountains and plains, and they haven't finished the job yet, even after 2,000 years. Bless them, they're still working at it. They get a bit discouraged sometimes when Lucifer leans on them extra hard, but the Spirit of the Mighty One inside them keeps them from giving up completely.[4]

Yes, you at the back, you had a wing in the air? You want to know why the Mighty One hasn't used angels to evangelize the world. Well, it's easy to think that we could have done it in far less than 2,000 years, with our greater strength and intelligence – not to mention our impressive appearance. But don't forget the age-old problem of their gift of choice. Those human minds are so twisted that however many angels might appear to them, if they don't *want* to believe they'll simply refuse to do so. Yet they are always impressed when an ordinary human, like themselves, tells them, 'I've found the secret of happiness. I used to be in such a miserable mess, but since I met God personally I ...' Yes, one enthusiastic Earthling, talking from experience, is worth thousands of angels, because we don't know what it feels like to be forgiven and changed by the Mighty One's love. So He has to rely on them – with all their obvious limitations.[5]

He needs us too – there's absolutely no danger of angels becoming redundant! There are still daily battles in the air with Lucifer's soldiers; and we are a vital part of the Mighty One's dealings with Earth.[6] He still sends us off to deliver messages through appearances, thought-plants or dreams, and we are always being sent by Him to strengthen, protect, accompany and guide His Lighted Ones who, nowadays, are even more important because they are each a temple where the Ruler of the Universe Himself resides.[7]

Quite early on, the 11 apostles infuriated the same Jewish leaders who had so recently hounded the High Prince to the cross. These men had them all put in jail while they mustered a full meeting of the council for the following day. During the night, a leading angel was sent down to open all the prison doors and set the Lighted Ones free. Early next morning, all the important men in the land gathered in their best clothes, and soldiers were sent to the prison to fetch the apostles for trial. The soldiers soon came hurrying back, looking very crestfallen, and reported that the prison doors were still locked, and the guards were in place outside them, but there were no prisoners in the cells. Just then someone ran in to say, 'Those men you arrested yesterday are preaching in the Temple – large as life!'

On another, most satisfying occasion, another angel helped Peter to break out of jail, the very night before he was due to die at Herod's hands.[8] No one was more surprised than the group of Lighted Ones who were pleading with God to rescue him! Honestly, we really do have to laugh! Prayer groups like that are made up of tiny creatures who look so powerless in comparison with the evil forces they are fighting, and most of them have pitifully little faith, yet it only takes a minute spark of faith on their part to change the course of our spiritual battles. Like I said before, they are the ones who decide which army wins. All they have to do is hold up their little faith shields, by prayer, against Lucifer's onslaughts, and all the power of Heaven is instantly released on their behalf. Lucifer uses all his energy keeping the knowledge of that fact from them and, to give him his due, most of the time he succeeds very well indeed!

There was another occasion around that time when another angel was sent to comfort a man called Paul during a shipwreck on his way to stand trial in Rome.[9] A wonderful man, that Paul was! He travelled round forming little clusters of Lights in cities all over the place.[10] He called them 'churches', and you'll find these Light-clusters all over the Earth nowadays. But here's a warning for you – while I remember it.

If you become Guardian Angels, never go volunteering yourself to look after a church – even if it feels like a big promotion. I've told you already that each Earth church has an angel in charge of it;[11] but those poor lads – what a dreadful job! Humans seem to be able to hurt one another more acutely in churches than anywhere else – except perhaps in their families.[12] They quarrel, criticize, struggle for power and use their church community to meet that need for importance that all humans seem to have somewhere in their make-up. They get so preoccupied with church politics and petty power struggles that they don't even realize that the Spirit of the Mighty One has left them and moved on somewhere else! And that is what He does, much to the deep sorrow of the angel who's left coping with all those self-important little turkey cocks!

I think I did tell you about the Evangel Angels, didn't I?[13] Unlit Earthlings do not have Guardian Angels – they don't even *want* them – but Evangels are used to introduce them to the Mighty One. On one famous occasion, one of them gave Peter's name and address to a Roman centurion[14] who wanted to know the Mighty One. This Evangel then helped that dear, but extremely bigoted, fisherman to realize that it was not *only* Jews whom the High Prince had died to save. There was another Evangel who's very highly honoured up here in Heaven, and I think his story will help you to understand their work better than any explanations from me.

Not long after the High Prince of Heaven had returned home, there was a great African Empress called Candace.[15] She had a very fine Chancellor of the Exchequer – a nobleman of the highest intelligence who served her excellently. This man had an unusually deep hunger in his soul for the Mighty One. You won't often find high-ranking statesmen, or very rich men, with a spiritual dimension to their lives. They have so many good things in this life that they don't crave Heaven. But this man was different. He wasn't a Jew, so he'd never been taught much about the Mighty One, but he had an unusually open mind. The Evangel in charge of his case managed to convince the Chancellor to take a trip to Jerusalem. It was a huge undertaking to travel so far, and the Empress Candace insisted that he took the best part of an army to keep him safe on the way.

When he arrived, he hurried straight to the Temple, hoping to meet God, but instead he met all the religious leaders, whom Lucifer still controlled. They bowed, scraped and flattered, and they pocketed his money. They talked business investments and trade pacts, but they never mentioned the God whom he had come so far to find.

After a few days the poor man became most frustrated; yet all the while his Evangel was trying to bring Lighted Ones near enough to speak to him. Earthlings usually think these 'chance' meetings are simply coincidences; they don't know how hard we angels work to make them happen! Perhaps an Evangel will be told to plant a name and address in the mind of a Lighted One and to suggest that they contact that person. The trouble is, Lighted Ones so often ignore angelic nudges like that, telling themselves they're imagining things!

It was particularly hard for that Evangel because there were so few Lighted Ones left in Jerusalem at that time. Most had fled for their lives, or even been shut up in prison by the worst Pharisee of them all, a young man called Saul.[16] (When his spirit was finally lighted, he became none other than that man Paul I've just been telling you about.)[17]

The handful of Lighted Ones who were left in the city had to be extremely careful. Still, that hard-working Evangel managed to set up several promising 'chance encounters', but every time the Ethiopian was beginning to talk to a Lighted One, round the corner would come one of those Pharisees, with a Lucifer agent on his shoulder. He'd offer an invitation to dinner or produce something he wanted to sell, and the Lighted One would have to melt hastily into the crowd.

The frustration! That poor Evangel was blocked at every turn. Really the job of an Evangel is most trying! However many times they manage to get their charges into situations where they hear how much God loves them, Earthlings can still go on refusing to respond, right to the very point of their death.[18] I couldn't work in that division! You should see the way they look when they have to watch the spirits they've been working with finally dragged away, out of their reach for ever, into the ghastliness below. It takes them a long time to get over the experience, I can tell you. When you get to Earth you're often going to hear Lucifer telling the Earthlings that a God of love could never send anyone to hell. But the Mighty One *never* sends anyone there, they *choose* to go – and just you remember that!

When the Ethiopian's stay in Jerusalem was over, he set off in his carriage to travel those thousands of miles home to Africa – thoroughly disappointed. All his Evangel's hard work and planning seemed to have been for nothing, but the angel simply refused to give up. Before leaving Jerusalem he had gently drawn the Chancellor's attention to a scroll in a bookshop near the Temple, and then made him feel 'compelled' to buy it. As the chariot bowled across the desert, he planted a thought in the Chancellor's mind: 'I feel bored. I wish I had something to read. Why don't I take a look at that parchment I bought in Jerusalem?'

I've seen Evangels draw the eyes of their charges towards a copy of the Bible, or encourage them to open a bedside drawer in a hotel or hospital and discover a Bible that a Lighted One had previously hidden there. Just reading the Mighty One's words is often enough to ignite a spirit.

The Chancellor of Ethiopia ordered his servants to find the scroll in his baggage, and he began to read it aloud to himself as his chariot bounced across the desert road. It was the book of Isaiah – the one our Scholarly friend is always quoting. Before the Evangel could become too pleased with himself the Scholar Angel called down to him and said, 'He'll never understand it without a bit of help.' The Evangel looked dashed, but instantly another Evangel was beside him.

'Its all right,' he said. 'The Mighty One saw this need some weeks ago, and He sent me to arrange for a Lighted One called Philip to be here at exactly the right moment, to explain the book to your charge. Look, here he comes now.'

Philip was one of the 12 original friends of the High Prince; and a few weeks before, he had been having a marvellous time lighting up thousands of spirits by his preaching in a town called Antioch.[19] He had looked somewhat put out when an angel whispered a map reference in his ear and told him to get there – fast.[20] But he had learnt that faith and obedience please the Mighty One a lot more than a success-ful ministry, so he went without a murmur.

While Philip was trudging through the desert he, too, was probably wondering if he had been imagining things. At first the chariot looked like a tiny cloud of dust on the horizon but, as it drew nearer, the Holy Spirit told Philip to go over and see how close he could get to it. Fortunately, Philip was in peak physical condition, because he had to run beside that carriage for a long time before the statesman noticed him. Philip could hear the man reading aloud, but he was frowning and looking most confused by the description of the way the High Prince had been treated and the details of the horrible way He died.

'Who is this Prophet talking about,' muttered the Lord Chancellor, 'himself or someone else?'

Philip managed to shout, 'Do you understand what you're reading about, sir?' Most Earthlings wouldn't have been able to say anything while running that fast – their bodies are so ridiculously limited!

'How can I understand unless someone explains it?' replied the Ethiopian crossly. 'Let me give you a lift. I can see you're a Jew, so perhaps you could explain this book to me as we go along.'

Philip looked highly relieved and, as he sank into his soft seat, the Evangel and Philip's Guardian danced with glee above the carriage.

When Philip had finished telling the Chancellor the whole story of God's secret plan, the African exclaimed, 'Look, we're coming to an oasis – see the palm trees? There's bound to be a pool of water. Is there any reason why I shouldn't be baptized?'

Usually at baptismal services the candidates have a whole crowd of friends round the pool cheering them on, but this man had no one – that he could see. Little did he know that he was proudly watched by his new Guardian, freshly sent from Heaven, and by lots of other angels celebrating ecstatically, as we always do after a spirit is ignited.

Yes, we had fun that day, and our enjoyment was increased hugely by the sight of Philip being snatched out of the water by four big angels and carried, still dripping wet, to a place called Azotus where there were lots more people waiting to hear the message.[21] The Chancellor rode on home full of joy, but without realizing what an important part angels had played in his life. Soon there were many Lights burning all over Ethiopia.

We often hear Earthlings say sadly, 'There weren't any angels in the story of how I found God,' but there always are! In spite of that obvious fact, it will probably astonish you to know that frequently during the last 2,000 years Lighted Earthlings have decided that we angels no longer exist! Yes, I know it's extremely insulting when we have to work so hard looking after them all through their lives, but remember that it's just not done to complain to the Mighty One about His friends, however idiotic most of them may seem.[22] Lucifer is constantly criticizing and putting them down in front of the Mighty One – we certainly don't want to do his job for him!

✸

Yes, 2,000 Earth years have passed by since the High Prince became a baby, and we angels have gone on helping the Mighty One in just the same ways as we have since the beginning of time. Of course, our responsibilities have increased massively with the sharp rise in Earth's population, and modern technology means that we have to accompany our charges round the planet – and even the universe – at astonishing speeds. Not that we mind that, of course, but a slower method of transport, particularly walking, gave them so much more time to think and saved them from making many stupid mistakes.

The Others have been working flat out over the years, too. Every now and again Lucifer has launched an all-out attack on Lighted Earthlings. His agents have infiltrated the minds of power-hungry dictators and planted such irrational hatred that awful persecutions have swept the world. There was Nero, for instance, a Roman Emperor who, if he wasn't feeding Lighted Ones to lions for his friends' entertainment, was covering Christians with pitch and using them as torches to illuminate his parties. Over the years Lucifer's managed to have the Mighty One's followers starved, beheaded, beaten, imprisoned, driven from their homes, burnt at the stake and tied up at low water and then slowly drowned as the tide came in. If Lucifer had done all that to Earthlings himself, the rest of humanity would have united against him and risen up in protest, but he's far too clever for that. He managed to put religious groups up against one another, inciting them into large-scale sectarian killing and cruelty, while convincing each that they were doing God's will! Mankind's natural intolerance and self-righteousness played into his hands every time. You should have seen the disgusting things those Crusaders did, while the rest of Christendom called them heroes!

Strangely, these times of terrible suffering actually produced more Lights than they snuffed out, and suddenly Lucifer discovered that his best strategy was to make Christianity fashionable and respectable. Igniting the spirits of other people is extremely difficult for Lighted Ones when Lucifer's agents are telling people that they can earn the right to Heaven by attending church services and looking saintly in public.

I'm sad to say that the darkness on Earth has become very intense at times, and Lucifer's Lot often seem to be winning the war. You'll find it really upsetting to watch humans using that dratted gift of choice and *deliberately choosing* to reject the Mighty One. I just don't know how He manages to put up with the pain of it, but every hundred years or so He allows Himself a supernatural intervention. He sends down a massive cloud of Evangels to hit specific areas of the Earth – men call the phenomenon a 'revival'. These angels are given vastly increased powers for a short time. Supernatural healing, miracle interventions and appearances become far more frequent, but it is usually the spirit of repentance they pour over humans that causes the greatest stir. This causes men to weep over their sins with no apparent human prompting, while others fall flat on their faces in the streets or at church in awe at the Mighty One's Majesty. Angels are also ordered to gather huge crowds to hear preachers like Wycliffe, Huss, Luther, Wesley, Moody and Billy Graham and then, while Warriors fight off the enemy, they open men's hearts to the Prophet's message. Yes, whole nations have been saved from Lucifer by these revivals and the whole course of human history has been changed by them. But most of the time the work of Evangels is a long, hard slog, simply because there are so few Lighted Ones who are willing to help them. All the same, we have watched some brave little people with frail bodies but blazing spirits leaving home and family and setting off into jungles, deserts, bandit-infested mountains, frozen wastelands, uncharted waters and dark forests, simply to tell other Earthlings how they can live for ever. Their Guardians were so proud of them!

*

At this point I feel I must pay a special tribute to that great Warlord – the Archangel Michael himself – for his magnificent achievement in preserving the Jewish nation for thousands of years. His fight with Lucifer's Persian toady in the days of Daniel[23] was nothing in comparison with some of his more recent battles. Over and over again, ever since the Mighty One made His special pact with Abraham, Lucifer has planned ways of destroying the Jews completely; and he never seems to have much bother getting his human servants on Earth to help him either. The poor Jews have been hounded, tortured and sent off to numerous death camps. In the memory of living Earthlings, six million of them were wiped out by one of Lucifer's favourites, Adolph Hitler. That nasty little man was ruled by an exceedingly powerful demon prince who was one of the Cherubim before the Fall. Michael and his Warriors very nearly lost, but Lucifer actually went too far in the end. The rest of Earth's nations were so revolted by what Hitler had done that the Jews were given their land back again – after 2,000 years – and these days they're doing very nicely, thank you! Lucifer is wild.

Yes? I see another wing at the back? Why are there still so few Lights down there, if the Mighty One is actually living on Earth Himself? Well, that's the tragic core of Earth's story. It's still Lucifer's planet and he's very artful! He uses all kinds of devices to stop Lighted Ones co-operating with Evangels. He'll either encourage them to become so enthusiastic that they rapidly burn themselves out with overwork, or he 'blindfolds' them so that they don't seem to see all the people around them who do not know that their Creator loves them, simply because no one has ever told them so.[24] He gets them scuttling off to Christian meetings like self-important ants, or encourages them to become so busy developing powerful ministries and taking on important church leadership roles that they never manage to ignite the spirits of their friends and neighbours. Their smugness and self-importance is so unattractive, you see. Lucifer is delighted if he can manage to make them live without joy or a skip in their step, because they just don't realize that the Mighty One adores them and longs for them to revel in His love – to dance exuberantly in it and share it with others. Lucifer is constantly hiding from them the fact that the Mighty One wants them to be happy! If He wanted them to be nothing but servants, He certainly would never have created them in the first place. He already had us angels – and we're far more efficient servants than Earthlings could ever be. No, He created them for love – that is their highest calling – but Lucifer sees to it that only a tiny handful have ever realized that.

No, I'm sad to say that it's not surprising that there are so few Lights down there on Earth; and, at the moment,

Lucifer's disgustingly pleased with himself because he's managed to get the world into the worst mess ever. Disgusting things are happening and the stench of misery caused by humans breaking the Ten Rules of Happiness is so revolting that Watcher Angels have to hold their noses![25]

✱

Now why are some of you looking so miserable? Angels are supposed to be full of joy too – remember? Oh, you think you were created too late, and you've missed all the excitement. Well, you're wrong there! Lucifer's time is fast running out – he's gone too far, just like he always does. Human beings will soon destroy themselves – and their planet – unless someone stops them; and that is exactly what the Mighty One is going to do.[26]

No, the biggest excitements of all are just about to happen, and the High Prince will soon be returning to Earth. We angels are not too sure of the exact details[27] – except, of course, for our Scholarly friend, who is *sure* he knows *all* the Mighty One's plans. He says they're all written down in the Great Book, but as far as the rest of us can see, the Mighty One has scattered bits of His plans all through His Book like pieces of an Earthling's jigsaw puzzle. One day we'll look back and see them all fitting together to form a clear picture, but until then all that we and Earth's theologians have are a load of fragments hidden all through the Book. One thing we do know for sure, because the High Prince said it so often, is that we angels will be deeply involved in everything which happens. He told us we'd all be with Him when He suddenly appears in the skies above the Earth.[28] He also said no one down there would be expecting Him – and things would be blacker than ever before.[29] Michael will be commanded to shout the command, and the trumpeters of Heaven will sound the greatest fanfare of all time.[30] Everyone on Earth will see the High Prince, and billions of us will appear in the sky with Him – wave upon wave of brilliant angels.[31] Oh, what a time we'll have!

The Lighted Ones who are already safe in Heaven will come with us too, to see the fun, and Michael's Warriors will be sent all over the Earth to collect up all the other Lighted Ones who are still alive at the time.[32] They'll be caught up by the angels to meet the High Prince in mid-air. Oh, what a party we'll all have together![33]

The next job the Warriors will be given is definitely *not* so nice. They'll be despatched to round up everyone who persistently rejected the Mighty One's love and deliberately turned away from Him.[34] These people will be handed over to the terrible satanic angel Apollyon, who rules the Abyss, who will keep them imprisoned until the final Day of Judgement.[35]

I guess Michael will enjoy his next responsibility a lot more. He'll be sent from Heaven with a great chain in his hand to arrest Lucifer, bind him and imprison him and all his followers in the same ghastly Bottomless Pit to wait until the Mighty One is ready to deal with them.[36] It's such a horrible place that I almost feel sorry for them! I did say *almost*.

Meanwhile, back in Heaven the High Prince and His Lighted Ones will be enjoying the greatest banquet of all time.[37] It will be His Wedding Feast. Even though there will be millions of them sitting at table with Him, each one will feel they have His undivided attention, and their relationship will be intimate and close like that of a bride and groom. We angels will serve the meal and provide the music and dancing for their entertainment. Oh *how* we're all going to enjoy seeing our Prince so happy with all the ones He loves safely around Him![38] The joy in the hearts of His 'Bride' will be indescribable too, as they join us angels after supper in worshipping the One we all honour so highly.[39]

Then will come the Great Prize-Giving ceremony when the rewards earned by the Lighted Ones during their stay on Earth will be given out by the Mighty One Himself.[40] Based on the records kept so carefully by the Recording Angel, their future responsibilities will be assigned. You see, the High Prince of Heaven will use them to help Him govern the Earth when he goes back down again.[41] And, after the celebrations are all over, that's just what He's planning to do.[42]

Because of all the disasters which will have happened down there,[43] only a small number of humans will still be alive, but He will care for these people and comfort them after all the dreadful traumas they have witnessed, and He and His Lighted Ones will help them to clear up all the mess which wars and plagues have left on the Earth. He will be their King, and suddenly Earth will become a lovely place, full of peace and ruled by love.[44] Even the leopards and bears will sleep curled up beside lambs and little Earthling children, and all the creatures the Mighty One created will respect and value one another at long last. The Lighted Ones will each be assigned a district to rule for Him.[45] The size of their domain will vary according to how they proved themselves in their previous life.[46] We angels will help them, and it may sound strange to you now, but in those days they will be higher in rank than we are, and we will count it a privilege to serve them in any way they desire.[47]

Total happiness will cover the Earth for a thousand years, and everyone will keep the Ten Rules of Happiness.[48] There will be no demons there to spoil things, you see. Our

Scholarly friend insists that after a thousand years the Mighty One will give Lucifer and his Lot one last chance, and Michael will be told to set them free for a while.[49] The very thought of it makes us angels shudder, but the High Prince's subjects, who have been born during the thousand years of His rule, must be given the chance to choose between Lucifer and Jesus – good or evil, light or darkness.

Terrible battles are in store for the entire universe at that point because Lucifer is *not* likely to give in easily, but it will be the High Prince Himself who wins the last great battle on the field of Armageddon.[50] He and Lucifer will meet face to face and, at long last, that great scoundrel will have to admit defeat. For the last time Michael will be told to take him by the scruff of his grubby neck and chuck him down into the terrible furnace called the Lake of Fire, along with all his followers.[51] There will be no more chances for any of them then.

Earthling children love their stories to end with the words, 'and they all lived happily ever after.' But in life on Earth that never happens. In Heaven it does. After all the upheavals, wars, struggles and strife, we angels, the Lighted Ones and our wonderful God will certainly live happily ever after.

So all of you new angels can look forward to some wonderfully exciting experiences in the future.

But now, pick up your harps, unfurl your wings, and ... *dismiss!*

Notes

1. Acts 17:28.
2. Isa. 42:8–9.
3. Ps. 19:3–4.
4. 1 Pet. 5:8–10.

5. 'Do you realize how fortunate you are? Angels would have given anything to be in on this!' (1 Pet. 1:12b, *The Message*).
6. Eph. 6:10–12.
7. 1 Cor. 3:16.
8. Acts 12:1–19.
9. Acts 27:27.
10. 2 Cor. 11:27–29.
11. Rev. 2:1.
12. 1 Cor. 3:1–4.
13. Job 33:14, 23–30.
14. Acts 10:1–8.
15. Acts 8:26–40.
16. Acts 8:1–3.
17. Acts 9:15.
18. Mark 10:17–22.
19. Acts 8:5–7.
20. Acts 8:26.
21. Acts 8:40.
22. 2 Pet. 2:10–11.
23. Dan. 10:20–21.
24. Rom. 10:12–15.
25. Rom. 8:22.
26. Isa. 10:3–4; Rom. 2:5.
27. Matt. 24:26.
28. Matt. 16:27.
29. Luke 21:9–26; Acts 2:19–21.
30. Matt. 24:31.
31. Matt. 25:31; 2 Thess. 1:7.
32. 1 Thess. 4:15–17.
33. Luke 21:27.
34. Matt. 13:41, 49; 25:41; Jude 13–15.
35. Rev. 9:1–2, 11.

36. Rev. 20:1–3; 14:10; 2 Pet. 2:4.
37. Rev. 19:17.
38. Heb. 12:22–23; Rev. 5:11–13.
39. Rev. 5:11–13.
40. 1 Cor. 3:12–15.
41. Rev. 2:26; 1 Cor. 6:2.
42. Rev. 20:4.
43. Rev. 8:6–13; 9:15, 18.
44. Isa. 2:4.
45. Rev. 20:4.
46. Luke 19:17–19.
47. 1 Cor. 6:3.
48. Isa. 11:9–10.
49. Rev. 20:3.
50. Rev. 16:14, 16.
51. Rev. 20:10.

Also available from HarperCollins by Jennifer Rees Larcombe

No hands but ours

Gestures of love aren't all about grand shows of affection. Sometimes what we need more than anything is simply a kind word, a hug or someone who will listen to us when we need to share our troubles.

Jennifer Rees Larcombe's classic book – now completely revised and updated – shares her experiences of learning to be 'God's gloves' and expressing His love not in fine words but in simple gestures and deeds.

By learning to be sensitive and open to others, we can indeed be used by God to bring help, hope and kindness into people's lives. Showing our compassion for those around us is one of the simplest, yet greatest ways of demonstrating the utter, personal love Jesus has for every one of us.

Books for children

Auntie Peggy's Windmill and other stories

These beautiful stories from Jennifer Rees Larcombe capture the adventures of childhood, but also the difficulties, helping children understand where strength can be found for the good times and the not-so-good.

Auntie Peggy's Windmill is the story of Emma and David's holiday with their eccentric aunt. She burns the toast and feeds them chocolate biscuits for breakfast, but she also teaches them about why she talks to God.

The Park People is a collection of stories revolving around the children who live near the park. With all kinds of interesting characters – Hetty the horrible dog, Alice whose Mum paints pictures, and Sam who nearly has an unhappy birthday – the book rings true to life, the unique people we meet and the varied lives we live.

Best Bible Stories

Illustrated by Steve Björkman

The Terrible Giant
Everyone is terrified of Goliath, the biggest man in the world. He is so fierce that not even the King of Israel or his army will fight him. Then a brave young shepherd boy arrives with a sling and a stone. Can he really stop the giant? But David is not afraid – he knows God is with him.

The Boy Who Ran Away
Jesus wants people to know how much God loves them, so he tells a story about a boy who runs away from his family. The father in this story is just like God – if we really are sorry, he throws his arms open wide and welcomes us back.

The Baby in the Basket
The Princess of Egypt is most surprised to find a baby boy in a basket on the Nile. Who is this baby, and why have his family hidden him? Close by is his big sister. She knows the answers! Will the Princess rescue this special baby? It's all part of God's great plan.

The Man Who Was Not Tall Enough
Zacchaeus has lots of money but people don't like him because he's greedy. When Jesus comes to town, everyone rushes to see him, but he won't talk to a mean little person like Zacchaeus – will he?

The Children's Bible Story Book

Illustrated by Alan Parry

The Children's Bible Story Book draws together a masterful partnership of authorship and illustration to tell in words and pictures 100 great stories from the Bible.

The aim of the book is to tell the whole story of the Bible chronologically, to show God's great plan unfolding and to present the Old Testament and New Testament stories in a way that will appeal to children.

In the words of the author: 'I want above everything to make God real to children, not only by the character of Jesus Christ, but also through His dealings with the people of the Old Testament. I want them to realize how much He loves them and desires their love in return. After all, surely that is the story of the Bible.'

The language is such that children of all ages will delight in the stories; younger ones will enjoy having the stories read to them, and older ones will enjoy reading the stories for themselves.